OMAR KHAYYAM
THE RUBAIYAT
A SELECTION

The Original Persian Text
and
A Literal Translation and an Introduction

by

Parvine Mahmoud

A HEARTHSTONE BOOK

CARLTON PRESS CORP.
NEW YORK

AUTHOR'S NOTE

THIS IS a second edition of my book: Omar Khayyam, *The Rubaiyat, A Literal Translation* (Tehran: San'at Rooz, Kashani Press, 1969). This new edition presents a selection of the *Rubaiyat*, with additions to the Introduction, and a few changes in the translation section.

CONTENTS

We are all dust, play the harp, O Saqi
We are all wind, bring the wine, O Saqi

PREFACE

Presenting a new, literal translation of the *Rubaiyat* of Omar Khayyam, an Iranian poet, astronomer, mathematician, and philosopher of the late eleventh century and early twelfth century, necessitates a rather difficult decision. Which one of the available manuscripts or Iranian editions of the quatrains should be used? Great discrepancies exist between the various manuscripts and editions, pointing to the fact that quatrains by other poets who imitated Khayyam, have been included in them. The search for the authentic quatrains has been continuous since 1859 when Edward FitzGerald published his paraphrased English "verse rendering" of the *Rubaiyat*, and attracted the attention of scholars to Khayyam's poetry.

FitzGerald used a manuscript written more than three centuries after Khayyam's death—the Bodleian 525 dated A.H. 865 (A.D. 1460–1461). The search produced other manuscripts, among them the Chester Beatty manuscript dated A.H. 658 (A.D. 1259–1260) and the Cambridge manuscript dated A.H. 604 (A.D. 1206–1207). The circumstances of these discoveries have been explained by Arthur J. Arberry in the introduction of his book *Omar*

Khayyam (New Haven: Yale University Press, 1952).

The discovery of the Chester Beatty and the Cambridge manuscripts may have increased the possibility of clarifying further the problem of the authenticity of the quatrains, but the progress, if any, to be made in that direction can be measured only after these manuscripts have been exhaustively studied. Until then, we cannot be sure of the authenticity of all the quatrains contained in them, and these two manuscripts raise therefore the same basic questions as did the previous manuscripts. Which quatrains were written by Khayyam, and which ones by his imitators? Which is the original text of Khayyam's quatrains? There are also variations in the text of the same quatrain presented in the manuscripts.

Since there have been no indications thus far of the existence of a manuscript of the *Rubaiyat* prepared by Omar Khayyam himself, it becomes clear that these questions cannot be answered with certainty, and some doubt will always remain. About Khayyam's imitators, however, the matter has been clarified to some extent, particularly by the Iranian scholar Mohammad Ali Forooqi, through the study of the characteristics of the style, rhythm, mood, and thought of Khayyam's poetry. This study has resulted in the elimination of quatrains that do not have his unique characteristics. But Khayyam's imitators were sometimes talented poets who imitated him to perfection, and consequently, even after careful study, a few quatrains by other poets may still be accepted as Khayyam's.

The absence of a manuscript by Khayyam himself leaves us facing the fact that the first transcriptions of the *Rubaiyat* must have been made from memory. We are therefore dealing with the process of oral transmission that invariably involves deviations from the original text. In the case of the *Rubaiyat*, the deviations must have been greater and more numerous than usual in oral transmission, owing to the lack of precision and care among Iranian scribes of those days who wrote down what they heard, and also because of the general practice among Iranians of supplying verses whenever their memory failed them. Other deviations may have entered the manuscripts because of the difficulties involved in reading the complicated and ornamented handwriting used, as well as through the difficulties inherent in the Persian alphabet where a single dot or a tiny dash are the only indication that two distinct letters are being used.

We may therefore conclude that it is basically impossible to state with certainty that any one of the manuscripts now available actually contains Khayyam's quatrains exactly as he wrote them. We can only say that these manuscripts vary in authenticity as a result of careful study and examination by scholars. It is with all these considerations in mind that I have turned to the Persian edition of the *Rubaiyat* by Mohammad Ali Forooqi and Qani (Tehran: Ranguin, A.H. 1321 [A.D. 1942]). Forooqi, an eminent Iranian scholar, spent a great deal of time in the study of Khayyam's poetry, examining manuscripts, searching for original quatrains in ancient books, and re-examining the findings of other scholars. He finally reached the conclusion that the best method of finding the authentic quatrains, with the highest possible degree of certainty, would be to determine the most characteristic traits to be found in Khayyam's poetry, and then, to examine each of the quatrains attributed to him, on the basis of those characteristics. To establish such a basis of testing, Forooqi searched for quatrains attributed to Khayyam by the most reliable historians, writers, and scholars from the times closest to that of Khayyam up to the present century. He succeeded in finding 66 quatrains that he considered authentic. After having determined the particular characteristics of thought, mood, style, and art appearing and reappearing in these 66 quatrains, Forooqi examined one by one all the quatrains contained in the most ancient manuscripts available, accepting or rejecting the quatrains on the basis of his already established criteria. Thus he selected 178 quatrains as being most probably by Omar Khayyam, and published the above-mentioned edition of the *Rubaiyat*. Of these 178 quatrains, 69 are found in the Chester Beatty manuscript, and 89 in the Cambridge manuscript.

In spite of that careful process of selection, there may still be a few quatrains that could appear unauthentic to some. However, since the Forooqi edition of the *Rubaiyat* seems to be the most authoritative at the present time, I have used it for my translation, and I have selected those quatrains that are, in my opinion, most representative of Omar Khayyam's style, poetry, and thought. I am presenting them here in the original Persian along with my literal translation into English, following Forooqi's numbering throughout.[1]

The introduction that follows presents Omar Khayyam as he emerges from the accounts of reliable historians and writers, as well as from his own writings, including the *Rubaiyat*. The introduction presents also a brief review of the time in which the poet lived. Finally, I have made an analysis, based chiefly on the quatrains, of Khayyam's thought and poetry.

The translation of the quatrains presented here is a literal one. No attempt has been made to translate Khayyam's poetry into English verse, since the demands of English versification, no mater how beautiful, inevitably distort the original. My intention has been to present the true voice of Khayyam, and this translation is as close to the true voice of Khayyam as the English language allows. Inevitably a great deal of poetic charm is lost in translation, but the rhythm of Khayyam's poetry is retained as much as possible, and no disruptive English verse rhythm is introduced. In short, I have tried to present the true Omar Khayyam, the man and the poet, as completely and as accurately as possible.

OMAR KHAYYAM
THE RUBAIYAT
A SELECTION

INTRODUCTION

THE TIME OF OMAR KHAYYAM

OMAR KHAYYAM lived during the second half of the fifth century, and the first half of the sixth century of the Hijrat (the eleventh and twelfth centuries of the Christian era), a time when the great kings of the Seljuqian dynasty ruled over the Middle and Near East. The Seljuq Turks were rude nomads and bold warriors, and after conversion to Islam, they became fervent Muslims. Their valor as warriors combined with a fanatical zeal for religion made them the lords of the Islamic Empire, and a great power in the world. It was they who repeatedly inflicted defeat upon the Christian Crusaders. The Seljuqs created one of the greatest empires known to history, and their time was a glorious epoch filled with brilliant achievements. Their empire reached its zenith under Sultan Jalal-id-Din Malik Shah, who was a great conqueror and a wise king. He administered justice in person and served the cause of religion. A man of culture, he sought the advancement of science and encouraged letters. It was he who in the year A.H. 467 (A.D. 1074–1075) established the observatory at Nayshaboor, and called upon Omar Khayyam and other eminent scientists to reform the calendar, thus inaugurating the Jalali era.

From the intellectual point of view, the Seljuq period was a brilliant one. Many important works, both in Persian and Arabic, were written during this time by a great number of poets, prose writers, philologists, geographers, historians, and commentators.

Nizam-ul-Mulk (1017–1092), the powerful vizir of the Seljuqs, was one of the dominant figures of his time. A great statesman, an able administrator, and a protector of sciences and letters, Nizam-ul-Mulk was the foremost builder of the glory and prosperity of the Seljuq empire. The vizier was also an eminent man of letters. His *Siyasat Nameh,* or *Treatise in the Art of Government,* is one of the most valued works in Persian literature. In his efforts to promote learning, Nizam-ul-Mulk created the Nizammiyyeh colleges that became famous throughout the Islamic world. These colleges had magnificent buildings, immense libraries, and living quarters for thousands of students. The teaching was entrusted only to the most eminent scholars.

The vizier's example was followed by Sultan Malik Shah and many other wealthy and influential men of that period, who also created new colleges and various centers of study. As a result, a great development took place in the field of education in all the provinces of the empire, and Khorassan, the native land of Omar Khayyam, became a great center of learning.

The main subject of study in those days was religion. The Seljuq kings, being fervent and fanatical Muslims, enforced orthodox Islam with great rigidity. Thus the theologians became very powerful during that period, and they had a great influence on the public. Rational sciences and philosophy were condemned by them and could not be taught in colleges and mosques. Those who studied these subjects were accused of heresy. Omar Khayyam, accused of being a philosopher, had to defend himself (see quatrain 129).

The question of religion was not a simple one. Because of the existence of numerous opposing sects, the discussions and controversies that stirred the intellectual atmosphere of that period often took dangerous turns and had violent consequences. From the assemblies of the theologians, clergymen, and students of religion, these debates spread first to their followers, and then, to the public. The issues became confused and exaggerated, causing riots and civil wars that destroyed towns— buildings and libraries were burned. These controversies were very serious since they concerned fundamental differences between the various sects of orthodox Islam and Shiism—the schism or heresy of Islam.

All the various schools of Islam were very active in debate, controversy, teaching, and propaganda. From the viewpoint of religious influence and political power, however, none could be compared to the sect of the Ismailis—one of the divisions of Shiism that played an important role during that period. The chief of the Ismailis was Hassan Sabbah, the famous Old Man of the Mountain, who captured the stronghold of Alamut in A.H. 483 (A.D. 1090–1091). Hassan Sabbah sought power through religion in order to satisfy his personal ambitions. Under his leadership, the Ismailis achieved not only great religious influence, but also political power—an immense power gained through the most violent forms of terrorism. Hassan Sabbah established the order of the Assassins who, at his command, murdered kings, ministers, and other influential men, spreading terror throughout Western Asia. These crimes, of course, were not left unpunished, and were followed by persecution and massacre of the Ismaili heretics by the orthodox. One can easily imagine the atmosphere of unrest, violence, and terror that prevailed during that entire period.

The time of Omar Khayyam was one of the great moments of history. In politics, a dynasty of powerful kings ruled over an immense empire. In the realm of knowledge, a glorious epoch witnessed an unprecedented development in all branches of learning. In literature, a brilliant era produced many great poets and prose writers. A time of intellectual effervescence indeed, but also one of intense religious controversy that brought violence and terrorism upon an otherwise prosperous society.

THE LIFE AND CHARACTER OF
OMAR KHAYYAM

FACTS ABOUT Omar Khayyam's life are scarce. He was born in Nayshaboor, a town in the province of Khorassan, in northeastern Iran. When was he born? When did he die? No one knows exactly. The year A.H. 517 (A.D. 1122–1123) has been suggested as the possible date of his death. It is certain, however, that he lived during the second half of the fifth century, and the first half of the sixth century of the Hijrat (the eleventh and twelfth centuries of the Christian era). Omar's nickname was Abul-Fathe (father of victory), his title of honor, Ghyass-id-Din (supporter of religion), but the writers of that time, refer to him as Omar, son of Ibrahim Khayyam ("Khayyam" meaning tent maker), and that informs us about his father's name. Omar probably spent the greatest part of his life in Nayshaboor where his ancestors had lived, and he is remembered today.[2]

What is certain about Khayyam is the fact that in the year A.H. 467 (A.D. 1074–1075), he was a member—a most eminent one—of the committee of scholars appointed by Sultan Jalal-id-Din Malik Shah, to reform the calendar. There is also, in Istanbul, a letter written to

Omar Khayyam by the poet Sanai. In this letter, the most ancient document which mentions Khayyam, Sanai asks Khayyam to intervene in his favor in an affair which he has been unjustly accused. This letter shows clearly the influence enjoyed by Khayyam in Nayshaboor.[3]

Historians and writers provide us with additional information about Omar Khayyam. They all speak highly of him, consider him a great scholar versed in all sciences, and praise his work and his scientific achievements—writers such as Abdul Rahman Khazeni, a contemporary of Khayyam, in his book *Mizan-ul-Hikmat* (Basis of Philosophy) written in the year A.H. 515 (A.D. 1120–1121); Zamakhshari in his treatise *Alzajir-ul-Sighar en Muarizat-ul-Kibar* (Defender of Children Against the Tyranny of the Elders) written probably before A.H. 538 (A.D. 1143–1144); and Nizami Aruzi Samarqandi in his book *Chahar Maqaleh* (Four Discourses) written about A.H. 550 (A.D. 1155–1156).

Nizami Aruzi, also a contemporary of Khayyam, in his above-mentioned book, in the Astronomers section, reports that in the city of Balkh, he heard Hujjat-ul-Haqq (Proof of the Truth) Khayyam say that his tomb would be in a spot where blossoms from trees would fall on it twice a year. Arriving at Nayshaboor in the year A.H. 530 (A.D. 1135–1136), a few years after Khayyam's death, he visited the tomb near the wall of a garden, and found it completely hidden under petals from nearby fruit tree blossoms. Nizami Aruzi relates also that Khayyam had chosen, for the Sultan who was going hunting, a few days during which there had been no clouds and no rain.[4]

In his book, *Nezhat-ul-Arwah* (Recreation of Souls)

composed in the thirteenth century, Shahrzuri gives more information about Omar Khayyam. He praises the intelligence and the memory of Khayyam who having read a book seven times while he was in Ispahan was able to transcribe it almost word for word, on his return to Nayshaboor. He presents Khayyam as a disciple of Avicenna, his contemporary, and reports that just before his death Khayyam was reading Avicenna's book, *Shafa*, saying: "O God! Verily I have striven to know Thee according to the range of my powers, therefore forgive me, for indeed such knowledge of Thee as I possess is my [only] means of approach to Thee."[5]

The opinion of Sheikh Najm-ud-Din Razi about Omar Khayyam is interesting. He considers him an atheist, a philosopher, and a materialist who recognizes his own perplexity. To support that statement, Razi cites two of Khayyam's quatrains. (See quatrains numbers 31 and 34).[6]

Qifti writes that Omar Khayyam taught Greek sciences. In his book *Akhbar-ul-Hukama* (History of the Philosophers) compiled in the second quarter of the thirteenth century, he also reports that the Sufis (Mystics), stressing the apparent meaning of Khayyam's verses, consider him a partisan of their system while with regard to religious law the true meaning of his verses is like stinging serpents.[7]

A few writers report that Omar Khayyam was a disciple of Avicenna. It is also known that he translated Avicenna's treatise on unity from Arabic into Persian.[8]

That is almost all the information we have about Omar Khayyam from these sources. In general he is presented as a great scholar, astronomer, mathematician, and mainly as an eminent scientist. Kings and lords held him in high esteem and had faith in his authority and learning. He was considered the equal of Avicenna. Theologians, however, accused him of being a philosopher and a free thinker.

The study of Omar Khayyam's own works provides us also with some information about him. In addition to Persian and Arabic poetry, he wrote several scientific and philosophical treatises that bear witness to his activities. A list of Khayyam's writings may be found in the Persian edition of his *Treatise on Algebra*.[9]

Omar Khayyam's works deal largely with scientific and philosophical subjects, but sometimes in an introduction he reveals some of his personal thoughts. In the introduction to his *Treatise on Algebra*, for example, after a brief history of that science, he speaks about his desire to engage in research, his inability to do so because of the vicissitudes of fortune, and the poor condition of scholars. He complains about the insincerity of his contemporaries, their love of materials things, and their contempt for honest men who search the truth.

These feelings show Khayyam's dissatisfaction with his time when theologians condemned rational sciences often for the purpose of preserving their influence. Khayyam deplores the lack of sincerity among his contemporaries who did not hesitate to use any means in order to gain power and influence. For example, those religious leaders, such as the Ismaili chiefs, who, with hypocrisy and deceit, made use of religion to advance their personal ambitions. In one of his quatrains, Khayyam deplores also the ignorance of the people whose stupidity makes them an easy prey for many a deceitful hypocrite:

There is a bull in the sky, and its name is Pleiades.
Another bull is hidden under the earth.
Open your wisdom's eyes. See, with certitude,
Under and above two bulls, a handful of
donkeys.

(144)[10]

The *Treatise on Existence*, written in Persian, is a scientific discussion of matter, essence, and related subjects. There is, however, in the third chapter of this treatise, a passage that reveals Khayyam's thinking. Speaking of those who seek to know God, he divides them into four groups: the Mutekaleman (a group of scholars of Islam), the philosophers and scholars, the Ismailis (a Shiite sect of Islam), and the Sufis (Mystics). Then, explaining the method of each group, he says that "the Sufis have sought knowledge by means of reflection, and, by purification of conscience and refinement of self from defects of nature and form, have followed this course, for when the purified essence faces the spiritual world, its true forms become apparent without any doubt, and that is the best of all methods, for it is clear to me that no perfection is better than exalted God."[11]

Another work by Omar Khayyam, the *No-Rooz Nameh*, was written, as Khayyam explains in the introduction, at the request of a friend. "No-Rooz" ("New-Day," i. e., New Year's day), is the ancient festival that marks the beginning of the Iranian year on the first day of the spring season. In this book, Khayyam explains the origin of the No-Rooz festival attributed to Jamshid, one of the famous kings of mythical Pishdadi dynasty of Iran. He discusses also other customs and legends of ancient Iran and talks about the marvelous and wise deeds of Iranian kings.

This desire to revive the days of Iranian greatness now gone, shown in the *No-Rooz Nameh*, seems to stem from the same feeling of nostalgia that inspired some of Khayyam's quatrains. Grieving over the annihilation that awaits every living thing, Khayyam, many times, evokes the ruins of the splendid palaces of ancient Iran and pictures the skulls of the great Iranian kings:

> I saw a bird perched on the rampart of Tus,
> Having laid before it the skull of Kay-Kavus,
> Saying to the skull: "Alas, alas! Where is
> The ringing of bells, and where the lament
> of drums?"

(114)

Living at a time when Iran was under the rule of the Seljuq Turks (a foreign dynasty), and the Iranian people were oppressed by their ruthless enforcement of Islam (a foreign faith, since Iranians were originally Zoroastrians), it is no wonder that Khayyam should long for the Iranian supremacy of the past. The nostalgia for an independent Iran was in fact a strong feeling among Iranians who had been for many years under Arab and Turkish rules. Thus the *No-Rooz Nameh* reflects this personal feeling of Omar Khayyam: his longing for an independent Iran.

It is perhaps in the *Rubaiyat* that Omar Khayyam's personality is most apparent. His sensitivity to the beauties of nature and his taste for the simple pleasures of life are reflected in many quatrains. Omar Khayyam enjoys the sight of fields abounding in tulips, the meadow where flowers bathe in the morning dew, the bank of the river covered with tender grass. Pure wheat bread and wine with a sweetheart among the greenery of a garden—these seem to him the most enjoyable feast. Above all, Khayyam finds pleasure in the contemplation of beauty. As he sits by the side of a field, he enjoys wine with a tulip-faced beauty. As he strolls in the moonlight, a cypress tall maiden walks along with him. As the spring clouds wash the flower bed, he receives a cup of wine from a sweetheart whose face kindles his heart.

In the *Rubaiyat*, some verses reveal that Khayyam has a proud nature, and that he likes dignity and independence:

> If a man could have bread for two days,
> And a drink of fresh water from a broken jug.
> The servant of a lesser man, why should one be?
> Or someone like oneself, why should one serve?
>
> (98)

The *Rubaiyat* also reveal Khayyam's thought and his poetic skill, a discussion of which follows.

THE THOUGHT OF OMAR KHAYYAM

In the Forooqi edition, the *Rubaiyat* open with the fol-
lowing quatrain which, as we shall see, summarizes
Khayyam's thought:

> Rise O beloved, solve our problem with your beauty.
> Bring, for (the comfort of) our hearts,
> A jug of wine that we may drink together,
> Before they make jugs from our clay.
>
> (1)

Human destiny is the main theme in the *Rubaiyat*. The
purpose of life and death. Why are we here? What is this
universe? What role does it play in our fate? Science and
religion fail to give satisfactory answers to these questions,
and Khayyam, himself a man of science, has no answers:

> Never has my heart been deprived of knowledge.
> Few secrets remain that have not been resolved.
> For seventy-two years, I reflected day and night.
> It became clear to me that nothing has been
> resolved.
>
> (93)

The answers presented by religion are not valid in the

eyes of Khayyam. Resurrection, future life, paradise, hell—no one can be sure they exist. Who has ever returned to tell us about death? Who has gone to hell? Who has come from paradise?

> How long will I mold bricks on the seas?
> I have grown weary of idol worshippers of synagogues.
> Khayyam! Who said there will be a hell?
> Who went to hell, and who returned from paradise?
>
> (21)

Khayyam does not accept illogical statements:

> Before being attacked by surprise, at night,
> Command that they bring the rose-colored wine.
> You are not gold, O heedless fool,
> To be put in the ground, and brought out again.
>
> (80)

Many tales are told about paradise and hell, about the heavenly houris[12] and castles, but Khayyam does not believe them (76). To those religious leaders who believe they are on the path of certitude, Khayyam says: "I fear that a voice may exclaim one day,/ O unaware people, the path is neither here nor there" (143). He shows the futility of their heated debates (127, 160), and takes delight in pointing out the contradictions in the teachings of theologians who promise in paradise the pleasures they forbid on earth:

> They say there will be paradise and houris.
> Wine, milk and honey will be there.
> If we chose wine and sweethearts, what fear?
> Since thus will be the outcome of the affair.
>
> (87)

Since no one has any knowledge of the truth (14), Khayyam would rather build a paradise here, on this earth, than wait for a paradise he may or may not reach (161).

In the face of the basic problems of human destiny, Khayyam recognizes our helplessness (82), and does not present vain explanations. Instead, he dispels false conceptions and presents facts. Using the scientific approach, he observes, examines, and draws conclusions. The universe, "that sea of existence," whose origin and purpose are unknown, is not considered by Khayyam a rational force that intervenes in human destiny. The "celestial wheel" seems to him as helpless as man, having no power over its own revolution (48, 172), and showing complete indifference to human fate:

> O friend, of truth, hear a word from me.
> Be with the ruby color wine and a silver-bodied (beauty).
> For he who made the world cares not
> For the moustache of someone like you, and the beard of someone like me.
>
> (162)

Moreover, Khayyam has no illusions concerning man. This being who considers himself immortal and above all creation is nothing but "dust, breeze, and breath" (23), or a drop of water that disappears into the sea (97). What of the passage of man through life? "A fly appeared and disappeared" (97). Does he have control over his fate? "Fill the cup of wine, for it is not clear to me,/ Whether this breath I inhale, I shall exhale or not" (155). Man knows nothing about his destiny, where he came from, where he will go (34), or what the purpose of his life is:

> Although beautiful color and scent are mine.
> A face like the tulip, and a stature like the cypress
> are mine.
> It is not known to what end, in the joyous feast
> Of earth, the eternal painter embellished me.
>
> (5)

Ignorance prevails in all these matters. Only one fact is certain, and that is death:

> The revolving world brings forth no flower from
> the earth,
> That it doesn't break, and deposit again in the earth.
> If clouds absorbed dust as they do water,
> Blood of dear ones would rain till resurrection day.
>
> (85)

But again, man knows nothing about death: "With cunning, I opened difficult knots,/ Each knot has been opened save the knot of death" (119), except that it is total annihilation: "These inhabitants of graves have turned into dirt and dust" (104).

Death is the great human tragedy in the eyes of Khayyam, and he is overwhelmed by the idea of this hopeless annihilation. He cannot accept death, and expresses, at times, a longing for a better destiny for man:

I wish there were a place for resting,
Or a destination to this long road.
I wish, after a hundred thousand years,
there were hope
Of springing, like grass, from the heart of dust.

(163)

Other times, Khayyam revolts against this injustice and wishes to have the power of God to build a new and just universe:

If I could, like God, lay hand on the celestial sphere,
I would eliminate this sphere.
Anew I would build another sphere,
So that a free man could easily fulfil his
heart's desire.

(145)

Khayyam, like many poets before and after him, is obsessed with the recurring theme of death. While contemplating life in its beauty and abundance, he sees death everywhere. That tender grass springs from the dust of a sweetheart (51), the tulip is red because it bathes in the blood of kings, and the violet was once a mole on the face of a lovely one:

Red tulips growing in every field,
Owe their color to the red blood of a king.
Every stem of violet springing from the earth,
Is a mole that was on a sweetheart's face.

(49)

Describing life with brilliant and gay colors, Khayyam's verses point out at the same time the constant presence of death threatening to destroy it at any moment. Many quatrains present this coexistence of life and death:

Saqi[13], flowers and grass have become much joyful.
Embrace the moment, for next week they will be dust.
Drink wine, pick a flower, for when you look again,
Flowers have become dust, and grass, motes.

(37)

Life is not only fragile, it is also short: "the duration of this world of dust,/ Is that of a wind that passes fast," (99), and this short life span, our lifetime, passes "like water in the stream, and wind in the field" (18). Soon we will be in "the heart of dust" (71).

Khayyam describes the life of man as "one borrowed instant in this corner of annihilation" (110). That one instant is our fragile and ever-threatened life, our only possession, our only capital. Why spend it in vain discussions? "Till when hopes and fears of an eternal or created world?" (127).[14] Why waste our life? "Spoil not this moment if your heart is not insane" (10). Why wait for a future life that no one guarantees? "A cup, a beloved, a harp, by a field,/ These three for me cash, for you, paradise on credit" (43). What we have, the only thing we surely have, is our present life. Khayyam constantly invites us in his poetry to enjoy it, for nothing guarantees its duration.

As we have seen, the threat of death and the enjoyment of life are the main themes of the *Rubaiyat*. The more we understand the tragedy of death, the more we realize the value of life. As we perceive more and more clearly the ever-present danger of death, it becomes more urgent to take advantage of this one short life given to us. We must enjoy it fully and now, "For this quarrelsome wheel suddenly one day,/ Will not give us time for a drink of water" (123). Above all, we must spend our life with joy, with tranquility, and forget our worries, for the wise have said: "The world's sorrows are poison" (158). Let us free our minds from restraint:

> The season of flowers, by a stream, alongside a
> field,
> With two or three congenial friends and a
> houri- natured beauty.
> Bring forth the cup, for the morning wine drinkers
> Are free from mosques, and indifferent to
> synagogues.
>
> (39)

Joy and tranquility, both necessary conditions for the enjoyment of life, are created by two things: beauty and wine. In the *No-Rooz Nameh*, speaking of the properties of a beautiful face, Khayyam says: "There are, in the world, many beautiful things, and seeing them gives joy to people, and refreshes their nature, but nothing can replace a beautiful face, for the joy that it produces surpasses all others. It is said that a beautiful face is the cause of happiness in this world."[15] Lovely-faced beauties abound in the *Rubaiyat:* "A face like the tulip," full of color and scent (5), "A face that kindles the heart" (19), "A moon–faced beauty" (116), "A paradise-faced beauty" (169). In their company, Khayyam leads us to refreshing spots of nature: "Amidst the meadow" (19), "by a stream" (39), to a field glittering with tulips (49), inviting us to enjoy the sight of the tender grass, the violet bending in the meadow, the rosebud gathering its skirt about it (92). Khayyam tells us not to put down the cup of wine, since to sooth the soul, there is nothing like wine:

> Drink wine, for it relieves (your) heart
> From all worries and pains in the world.
> Abstain not from an elixir of which
> A sip relieves a thousand ills.
>
> (90)

The state of forgetfulness and beatitude is represented in the *Rubaiyat* by the relaxation produced by wine—real wine that does not seem to be in any way symbolic. Khayyam believes in the beneficial properties of wine, and in the *No-Rooz Nameh* he relates the following story about its discovery:

> It is written, in history books, that in Herat, there was a successful and wealthy king with a great army. He ruled over the entire province of Khorassan. He was of the family of Jamshid [a legendary king of Iran]. His name was Shemiran, and he had a son, very brave, strong and manly, by the name of Badam. In those days, there was no better archer than Badam. One day, when the king was sitting in his gardens, with his son and all the dignitaries, it happened that a bird called Homay, a fabulous bird of good omen, flew in. The bird was crying as it landed in front of the king's throne. The king looked and saw around the bird's neck, a snake raising its head, and ready to sting the bird. The king cried out: "O you lion-hearted men, who

will free this bird from the grip of that snake?"
Badam said: "O king, that is my job." Then, with a
swift arrow, he nailed the snake's head to the
ground, without harming the bird which, freed
from the snake, few around for a while, then flew
away. The following year, on the same day, the king
was sitting in his gardens when the bird Homay
appeared again, flew around the king's head, and
landed on the same spot where the snake was killed
with an arrow. The bird dropped something from its
beak, cried a few times, and flew away. The king
asked his dignitaries whether they thought this was
the same bird Badam had rescued from the snake's
grip the year before, returning now to bring them a
gift. What the bird had brought was two or three
seeds. The king ordered his gardener to plant the
seeds deep into the ground to protect them from
birds. After some time, a plant grew on that spot. It
had large leaves, and bunches of small green fruit
hanging from its branches. It was a plant no one
had ever seen. When the fruit ripened, the king
came back to the garden and saw the green grapes
changed into ripe dark grapes, glittering like a
bride. Since the grapes were dropping, they thought
the main benefit of the fruit was perhaps in the
juice. So they poured the juice into a barrel, but no
one drank any of it for fear of being poisoned. When
the juice started to ferment in the barrel, the gar-
dener told the king that without any fire under it,
the juice was boiling. The king said to the gardener
to inform him when the boiling had stopped. The
gardener saw one day, that all was calm, and the
boiling juice had become clear and bright, shining
like a red ruby. The king was informed. He arrived

with all the learned men. They were surprised at the color and the clarity of the liquid. That is, they said, what this plant produces, but we don't know whether it is poison or not. Then, they brought a condemned prisoner and gave him a drink of that juice. He frowned for a while, but then he asked for more. After two drinks, he became cheerful, started to sing, the splendor of the king seemed light to him, and he wanted more of that drink. After the third drink, his head got heavy, and he went to sleep. The next day, when he woke up, they brought him before the king, and asked him what was it that he drank, and how did he feel. He said he didn't know what he drank, but he felt happy, and wished he could find three more cups of that same drink. The first drink, he said, was bitter, and I drank it with difficulty, but when it settled in my stomach, I wished for another one. After the second drink, joy and serenity invaded my heart, all modesty disappeared, and the world seemed light to me, I thought there was no difference at all between the king and me, my heart forgot all the world's sorrows. After the third drink, I went into a sweet dream. The king forgave the prisoner and set him free. All the learned men agreed that there was no greater gift than wine, since there is no food or fruit having the properties of wine. From then on, they made great quantities of wine, music, and songs. The garden where the seeds of grapes were first planted is still standing, and they say that grapevine spread from Herat to the rest of the world. [16]

That is the story told by Omar Khayyam about the origin of wine. It is a charming story. There is also in the *No-*

Rooz Nameh a chapter devoted to the usefulness of wine, and Khayyam enumerates its beneficial properties, explains at the same time its harmful effects, and gives methods for recovering from them. In the *Rubaiyat*, Khayyam often speaks of the good properties of wine:

Since Venus and the moon appeared in the sky,
Better than clear wine nothing has been seen.
I am surprised at wine merchants, for
Better than what they sell, what will they buy?

(73)

Wine is eternal life, it "burns like fire, but for sorrow,/ Soothes like the water of life" (108). "To live without clear wine, I cannot," says Khayyam, "and I am the servant of that moment when the Saqi says: 'Take one more cup,' and I cannot"[17] (132).

Beauty and wine being means, within our reach, to enjoy life by bringing about a state of forgetfulness and serenity, Khayyam repeats constantly that one must drink wine, forget all worries, and be happy:

Till when the tale of five and four, O Saqi?
Let it be one or a hundred thousand problems,
O Saqi.
We are all dust, play the harp, O Saqi.
We are all wind, bring the wine, O Saqi.

(168)

The immortality of the soul is questioned by Khayyam. He does not believe in it. For him, death is final, and there is no afterlife: "Drink wine, for I told you a thousand times before,/ There is no return, when you are gone, you are gone" (160). However, Khayyam suggests a different kind of immortality, a "material" immortality based on the principle of the subsistence of matter. The atoms that compose the human body become dust. Plants draw their food from that dust, and human atoms, therefore, participate in the life of plants:

> Every grass springing on the bank of a stream,
> Sprang, so to speak, from the lips of an
> angel–tempered beauty.
> So, do not step scornfully upon the grass,
> For that grass sprang from the dust of a tulip-faced
> beauty.
>
> (51)

But human atoms can also live again in another way. To make pots, the potter uses dust—the dust of human bodies. Atoms that were once part of a human body reappear in the body of a pot:

> I walked into the workshop of a potter.
> At the foot of the wheel, I saw the master standing,
> Molding on the pot a handle and a head,
> From the hand of a beggar, and the head of a king.
>
> (171)

Thus the human atoms start a new life that recalls their previous existence. Because of the similarity in the Persian language between the words for the opening, the neck, and the handle of a pot, and those for the mouth, the neck, and the hands of a human being, the pots lead a human life, and form a truly living world in Khayyam's poetry:

> This pot, like me, was a distressed lover,
> Caring for a sweetheart's locks.
> The handle you see on its neck,
> Is the hand that was around a sweetheart's neck.
>
> (15)

Filled with wine, the pots come to life. Wine becomes their soul (46), and communicates to their atoms a strange drunkenness. They remember, they whisper that they were kings and drank wine from golden cups (159). They ask the potter to treat them gently, for they were once like him (107). In the potter's shop, sitting motionless, two thousand in number, they seem to murmur in a hollow voice: "Where is the pot-maker, the pot-buyer, the pot-seller?" (117).[18]

Thus, even when man tries to forget his tragic destiny by drinking wine which brings forgetfulness, and by contemplating beauty which creates joy, he is still faced with the shadow of death. The jug of wine from which he drinks is made from the atoms of a desperate lover, and the verdure he contemplates, springs from the dust of a sweetheart. Khayyam insists on this constant presence of death to remind us of the importance of life. In the face of our cruel destiny, let us provide for ourselves a moment of happiness, not by taking refuge in dreams and illusions, but by seeing reality, and realizing the value of life. Let us enjoy this instant of life, "this one borrowed instant, in this corner of annihilation" (110).

We can see now that the opening verses of the *Rubaiyat* summarize perfectly Khayyam's thought:

> Rise O beloved, solve our problem with your beauty.
> Bring, for (the comfort of) our hearts,
> A jug of wine that we may drink together,
> Before they make jugs from our clay.
>
> (1)

It must be pointed out also that behind these subtle thoughts and beautiful poetry, Khayyam gives good advice on how to live wisely. One should try to lead a noble life, reject servitude, and have self-respect (98). Material things are not the sign of genuine greatness. Wealth and power do not last:

> That palace that emulated the (celestial) wheel,
> Against whose portal, kings put their faces,
> We saw a turtledove perched on its battlement, saying,
> Where (are they), where, where, where?
>
> (149)

To spend life gathering wealth, is an error (157). We cannot take it with us: "The seed of hope in the harvest will remain,/ The garden and the house, without you and me, will remain" (94). Let us be content with a simple, happy, active life (33, 77, 175). Let us seek knowledge (93), and the company of wise men (109), and strive only to acquire such qualities as self-reliance and dignity:

> To be content with a bone, like the vulture,
> Is better than to be a parasite at an ignoble man's table.

To be content with one's own barley bread, is
indeed better
Than to be contaminated with the sweet drink of a
mean man.

(142)

Let us not be hypocrites:

If you don't drink wine, don't taunt drunkards.
Don't engage in deceit and mischief.
Boast not that you don't drink wine.
You eat a hundred mouthfuls worse than wine.

(4)

Above all, let us not forget the great lesson taught by
death—the basic equality of all human beings. At the
end, kings and beggars alike will be dust and shaped
into pots (171).

The Poetry of Omar Khayyam

"R UBAIYAT" is the plural form of "rubai," the Arabic word for quatrain. The rubai is a special Persian verse form, and consists of two distichs or four verses. The first, second, and fourth verses must have the same rhyme. For the third verse, the poet may use the same rhyme or a different one. Often the poet tries even to end the first, second, and fourth lines of the rubai, with the same word or group of words. That is quite difficult to do, and is considered a special skill. Many of Khayyam's rubais have this structure. I have kept this special quality of his quatrains in my translation whenever possible, for example in rubais 19, 41, 116, 128, and others. This repetition of the same word or words, which occurs also inside the verses, plays an important role in the creation of the special rhythm of the rubai. The repeated use of the same word in a rubai is not, therefore, due to a lack of vocabulary or imagination. It is an intended device to produce a particular rhythm. For example, in rubai 45, instead of using two different verbs, "I asked," and "She replied," the poet uses the same verb, "I said," and "She said," which, in Persian, produces the desired rhythm: "Goftam" and "Gofta."

Because of its restrictive rules, the rubai is a difficult verse form. In four relatively short verses, the poet must express a complete thought, and the first three lines must prepare for the conclusion expressed in the fourth line. This requires precise thought, concise expression, and poetic talent and art. Omar Khayyam is considered one of the most talented poets in the composition of rubais. Each of his rubais is a masterpiece, combining poetic thought with delicacy of expression. Khayyam has also a rare talent for the special rhythm of the rubai that contributes a great deal to the beauty of the poetry in Persian, and this special rhythm is, without a doubt, the quality first lost in translation. There are also other qualities of these rubais that do not lend themselves to translation. The thoughts and the basic philosophy of the poet may be rendered with almost complete accuracy, but the art of expression, the aesthetic skill of the poet, and the rhythm of the poetry, can be appreciated only by those who read the *Rubaiyat* in the original. The true charm of Khayyam's poetry is the result of an artistic combination of Persian versification, rhythm, sounds, words, images, and moods. This poetic quality is in a unique equilibrium—an equilibrium that cannot be maintained when the elements that create it are changed through translation. The substitution of English equivalents for the Persian words disrupts the harmony and balance of the poem and destroys its special charm. One may attempt, however, to recreate the poetic atmosphere of the *Rubaiyat* by explaining the quality of both the rhythm and the thought, and by analyzing the sounds, moods, and images. That is what I shall attempt to do, but first to give some idea of the rhythm of Khayyam's poetry I shall transcribe with English letters the Persian text of one of the quatrains:

Har sobhe keh rooyeh laleh shabnam ghirad,

Balayeh banafsheh dar chaman kham ghirad.
Ensaf mara zeh ghoncheh khosh miayad,
Koo damaneh khishtan faraham ghirad.

(92)

Every morning when the dew covers the tulip's
face,
The violet's stature bends in the meadow.
Indeed I take delight in the rosebud,
For it gathers its skirt about it.

(92)

The word "ghirad" means "takes." In the first line, the face of the tulip "takes" the dew. In the second line, the stature of the violet "takes" a bend, and in the last line, the rosebud "takes" its skirt about it. The repetition of "ghirad" has a beautiful effect in Persian, because of its various shades of meaning. It provides also the special rhythm of this rubai.

As I have already pointed out, the thought expressed in a rubai must be concise and to the point. Khayyam being a scientist, in addition to being a poet, can and does successfully achieve remarkable results within the framework of the demands of his chosen verse form, the rubai. He conceives with precision. His thought is logical, his expression clear. Because of the subtlety of his selection of words, and his sensitivity to various tones and moods of expression, the quatrains contain suggestive words and expressions that enliven the thought with sounds, colors, and images. For example, the passage through life is underlined with the images of water running in the stream and of wind blowing in the field (18). Or the brilliance of a spring day is enhanced by the

sounds of the voiced syllables and by the colors of flow-
ers and grass. I transcribe the Persian once more, in the
hope that the reader will feel the sounds and the rhythm
of the poet's original language:

> Bar chehreh-yeh gol nasimeh No-Rooz khosh ast.
> Dar sahneh chaman rooyeh delafrooz khosh ast.
> Az dey keh ghozasht har cheh ghooy-i knosh nist.
> Khosh bash-o zeh dey maghoo keh emrooz khosh
> ast.

(19)

Khayyam enjoys the use of his native tongue in all its
subtlety and richness of vocabulary. Persian words are
harmonious and descriptive: *rooye* (face), *laleh-rooye*
(tulip-face), *may* (wine), *sarv-qad* (cypress-tall), *seem-tan*
(silver-body). Many times Khayyam repeats the sounds
of syllables to create special moods. In the workshop of
the potter where two thousand pots are sitting motion-
less, obsessed by the idea of death, Khayyam evokes this
obsessive atmosphere by the repetition of the soft sylla-
ble *koo*, which is the first syllable of the word *koozeh*
(pot), and which is also a word meaning "where is."
Rubai 117:

> Into the workshop of a potter, I walked yesterday.
> I saw two thousand pots speaking and silent.
> Suddenly one pot cried out:
> Where is the pot-maker, the pot-buyer, the pot-seller?

In another rubai, Khayyam uses *koo* for the same pur-
pose, imitating the cry of the turtledove:

Didim keh bar konghereh-ash fakhteh-i,
Benshasteh hami ghoft keh koo, koo, koo, koo?

(149)

We saw a turtledove perched on its battlement, saying,
Where (are they), where, where, where, where?

(149)

Vivid descriptions of nature enhance the poetic charm of the *Rubaiyat*. Like a skillful painter, Khayyam needs only a few rapid strokes of the brush to evoke a scene: "In the spring season, by a field" (35), "Flowers and grass have become much joyful" (37), "The season of flowers, by a stream, alongside a field" (39). With the same concision, poetic images are evoked: "Moonlight has torn, with light, the skirt of the night" (44), "How surprisingly (fast) life's caravan is passing!" (66). Other delicate images are presented in the following rubai:

O my heart, imagine all things in the world accord-
ing to your wish.
Imagine the garden of your joy embellished with
verdure.
Then imagine, upon that verdure, like dew,
You sat one night, and rose in the morning.

(103)

The main charm of the *Rubaiyat*, however, is to be found in the warmth of the atmosphere they create—an atmosphere of intimacy, human intimacy. In these qua-trains, man is a part of nature, all things have human quality. The cloud "weeps" on the verdure (8) and wash-es the dust from the flower-bed's "face" (79), precious gems (i. e., human bodies) lie in the "chest" of the earth (12), and every morning, the tulip's "face" is covered with dew, the violet's "stature" bends in the meadow (92), and the zephyr tears the "skirt" of the flower (154). This intimate atmosphere is created throughout the *Rubaiyat*. In these quatrains, Khayyam is conversing with the reader. He speaks directly to the reader: "Take in [your] hand [a cup of] wine, and a sweetheart's locks./ For this too will pass soon, and not remain long" (83). "O friend, come, let us not care for tomorrow" (121). "Sit in the shade of the flower" (154). "The field is like paradise, speak less of Kowsar" (169).[19]

Subtle thoughts, special rhythm, images, colors, sounds, and intimate tone all concur to give a rare poetic quality to the *Rubaiyat* of Omar Khayyam.

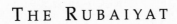

THE RUBAIYAT

1

Rise O beloved, solve our problem with your beauty.
Bring, for [the comfort of][20] our hearts,
A jug of wine that we may drink together,
Before they make jugs from our clay.

2

Since no one guarantees tomorrow,
For a moment, keep happy this grieved heart.
Drink wine in the moonlight, O beautiful,[21]
For the moon will often shine and not find us.

3

The Koran which is called the sublime word,
Is read from time to time, not perpetually.
Around the cup, there is a verse carved[22]
Which is continuously read everywhere.

4

If you don't drink wine, don't taunt drunkards.
Don't engage in deceit and mischief.
Boast not that you don't drink wine.
You eat a hundred mouthfuls worse than wine.[23]

حل کن بجمال خویشتن مشکل ما   برخیز بتا بیاد بهر دل ما

زان پیش که کوزه‌ها کنند از گل ما   یك كوزه شراب تا بهم نوش کنیم

۲

حالی خوش دار این دل پرسودا را   چون عهده نمی‌شود کسی فردا را

بسیار بتابد و نیابد ما را   می نوش بمهتاب ای ماه که ماه

۳

گه گاه نه بر دوام خوانند آنرا   قرآن که مهین کلام خوانند آنرا

کاندر همه جا مدام خوانند آنرا   بر گرد پیاله آیتی هست مقیم

۴

بنیاد مکن تو حیله و دستانرا   گرمی نخوری طعنه مزن مستانرا

صدلقمه خوری که می غلام است آنرا   توغره بدان مشو که می می نخوری

35

5

Although beautiful color and scent are mine.
A face like the tulip, and a stature like the cypress
are mine.
It is not known to what end, in the joyous feast
Of earth, the eternal painter embellished me.

6

We are with wine, and musicians, in this ruinous
corner,[24]
[Our] souls, hearts, cups, and robes, all full of wine.
Indifferent to hope for mercy, and to fear of tor-
ment,
Free from earth, wind, fire, and water.[25]

7

In the palace where Jamshid[26] held the cup,
The gazelle bore her young, and the fox rested.
Bahram who caught onagers all [his] life,
Did you see how the grave caught Bahram?[27]

8

The cloud came and wept again on the verdure.
Without the rose-colored wine, one should not live.
We are enjoying this verdure today,
Who will enjoy the verdure of our dust?

۵

چون لاله رخ وچو سرو بالاست مرا   هرچند که دنگ وبوی زیباست مرا

نقاش ازل بهر چه آراست مرا   معلوم نشد که در طربخانهٔ خاك

۶

جان ودل وجام وجامه پردرد شراب   مائیم ومی ومطرب واین کنج خراب

آزاد ز خاك وباد واز آتش وآب   فارغ ز امید رحمت و بیم عذاب

۷

آهو بچه کرد و روبه آرام گرفت   آن قصر که جمشید دراو جام گرفت

دیدی که چگونه گور بهرام گرفت   بهرام که گور میگرفتی همه عمر

۸

بی باده گلرنگ نمی باید زیست   ابر آمد و باز برسر سبزه گریست

تا سبزهٔ خاك ما تماشاگه کیست   این سبزه که امروز تماشاگه ماست

9

Now that the flower of your happiness is in full
bloom,
Why is your hand without a cup of wine?
Drink wine, for the world is a treacherous enemy.
A day like this is hard to find.

10

Today, for you, there is no access to tomorrow.
Thinking of tomorrow brings nothing but
melancholy.
Spoil not this moment if your heart is not insane,
Since it is not clear how much life remains.

11

O you arrived from the spiritual world of Taft,[28]
Perplexed in the five, four, six and seven,[29]
Drink wine since you don't know where you came
from,
Be happy! You don't know where you will go.

12

O celestial wheel, destruction is from your rancor.
Injustice is your old method.
O earth, if your chest should be opened.
Many precious gems[30] would be in your chest.

٩

اکنون‌که گل سعادتت پــرباداست   دست تو زجام می چرا بیکار است

مـی‌خورکه زمانه دشمنی غداداست   دریــافتن روز چنیــن دشوار است

١٠

امـروز تــرا دسترس فردا نیست   و انـدیشهٔ فردات بجز سودا نیست

ضایع مکن اینـدم اردلت شیدانیست   کاین بــاقی عمردا بهــا پیدانیست

١١

ای آمـده ازعـالم روحـانی تفت   حیران‌شده دردپنج وچهاروشش‌وهفت

می‌خور چـو نـدانی ازکجا آمدهٔ   خوش باش نـدانی بـکجا خواهی رَفت

١٢

ای چرخ فلک خرابی ازکینهٔ تست   بیـدادگری شیوهٔ دیــرینهٔ تست

ای خـاك اگـر سینهٔ تو بشكافند   بس گـوهر قیمتی که دردسینهٔ تست

13

O [my] heart, since the world makes you sad,
[And] your pure soul may suddenly leave your
body,
Sit upon the grass, and live happily a few days,
Before the grass springs from your dust.

14

This sea of existence has come out of the unseen.
There is no one who penetrated this gem of inquiry.
Everyone, out of fervor, said something.
Of what is, no one knows what to say.

15

This pot, like me, was a distressed lover,
Caring for a sweetheart's locks
This handle you see on its neck,
Is the hand that was around a sweetheart's neck.

16

This jug, the drinking cup of a wage-earner,
Is [made] of the eyes of a king, and the heart of a
minister.
Every wine bowl in the palm of a drunk,
Is [made] of the cheeks of a drunk, and the lips of a
virgin.

۱۳

ای دل چو زمانه میکند غمناکت   ناگه برود زتن روان پاکت

برسبزه نشین و خوش بزی روزی چند   زان پیش که سبزه بردمد از خاکت

۱۴

این بحر وجود آمده بیرون زنهفت   کس نیست که این گوهر تحقیق بسفت

هر کس سخنی از سر سودا گفتند   زان روی که هست کس نمیداند گفت

۱۵

این کوزه چومن عاشق زاری بوده است   در بند سرزلف نگاری بوده است

این دسته که بر گردن او می بینی   دستی است که بر گردن یاری بوده است

۱۶

این کوزه که آبخوارهٔ مزدوریست   از دیدهٔ شاهیست و دل دستوریست

هر کاسهٔ می که بر کف مخموریست   از عارض مستی و لب مستوریست

17

This old inn called the world,
The resting place of morning and evening,
Is a feast left behind by a hundred Jamshids,
A palace which is the refuge of a hundred Bahrams.[31]

18

These two, three days, [my] turn in life, have passed,
Like water in the stream, and wind in the field.
I never remembered the pains of two days,
The day that has not come, and the day that has passed.

19

Upon the flower's face, the No-Rooz[32] breeze is sweet.
Amidst the meadow, a face that kindles the heart is sweet.
When Dey[33] is passed, whatever you say is not sweet.
Be happy, and speak not of Dey. For today is sweet.

20

Before me and you, there were nights and days,
The revolving sphere was also at work.
Wherever you set foot upon the earth,
That [dust] was the pupil of a sweetheart's eye.

۱۷

و ادامگه ابلق صبح و شامست

این کهنه رباط را که عالم نامست

قصریست که تکیه‌گاه صد بهرامست

بزمیست که واماندهٔ صد جمشیداست

۱۸

چون آب بجوی بار وچون باد بدشت

این یک‌دو سه روزه نوبت عمر گذشت

روزی که نیامده‌است و روزی که گذشت

هرگز غم دو روز مرا یاد نگشت

۱۹

در صحن چمن روی دل افروز خوشت

بر چهرهٔ گل نسیم نوروز خوشت

خوش باش و ز دی مگو که امروز خوشت

از دی که گذشت هرچه گوئی خوش نیست

۲۰

گرنده فلک نیز بکاری بوده است

پیش از من و تو لیل و نهاری بوده‌است

آن مردمک چشم نگاری بوده است

هرجا که قدم نهی تو بر روی زمین

21

How long will I mold bricks on the seas?[34]
I have grown weary of idol worshippers of
synagogues.[35]
Khayyam! Who said there will be a hell?
Who went to hell, and who returned from paradise?

22

When a cup has been made,
A drunk would not consent to break it.
So many lovely heads and feet!
By whose love were they joined, by whose spite
broken?

23

Since the combination of elements favors you for a
moment,
Live happily, even if it is [like] poison to you.
Be with the wise, for the essence of your body
Is dust, breeze, mist, and breath.[36]

24

When the cloud at No-Rooz[37] washed the tulip's
face,
Rise and resolve upon a cup of wine.
For this grass that delights your eyes today,
Tomorrow, will all spring from your dust.

۲۱

تا چند زنم بروی دریاها خشت   بیزار شدم ز بت پرستان کنشت

خیام که گفت دوزخی خواهد بود   که رفت بدوزخ و که آمد زبهشت

۲۲

ترکیب پیالهٔ که درهم پیوست   بشکستن آن روا نمیدارد مست

چندین سروپای نازنین از سردست   برمهر که پیوست و بکین که شکست

۲۳

ترکیب طبایع چو بکام تودمی است   دوشاد بزی اگرچه برتو ستمی است

با اهل خرد باش که اصل تن تو   گردی و نسیمی وغباری و دمی است

۲۴

چون ابر بنوروز رخ لاله بشست   برخیز و بجام باده کن عزم درست

کاین سبزه که امروز تماشاگه تست   فرداهمه ازخاك تو بر خواهد رست

25

When the delirious nightingale flew into the garden,
Found the flower's face, and the cup of wine smiling,
He came and, in its own tongue, said in my ear,
Embrace the moment, for past life cannot be found
[again].

26

Since the world does not revolve according to a
wise person's wish,
Count the skies seven or eight[38] if you wish.
Since one must die and leave behind every wish,
Let ants eat [us] in the grave, or wolves in the field.

27

Like the tulip at No-Rooz, hold the cup in [your]
hand,
With a tulip-faced [beauty] if you have the chance.
Drink wine with joy, for this ancient wheel[39]
Will suddenly make you humble like dust.

28

Since there is no truth and certitude in hand,
One cannot wait, a lifetime, for a doubtful hope.
Beware that we do not put down the cup of wine.
In ignorance, what difference if a man is sober or
drunk?

۲۵

دوی گل وجام باده داخندان یافت   چون بلبل مست داه دردبستان یافت

دریاب که عمر رفته را نتوان یافت   آمد بزبان حال در گوشم گفت

۲۶

توخواه فلک هفت شمر خواهی هشت   چون چرخ بکام یک خردمند نگشت

چه مور خورد بگور وچه گرگ بدشت   چون باید مرد و آرزوها همه هشت

۲۷

با لاله رخی اگر ترا فرصت هست   چون لاله بنو روز قدح گیر بدست

ناگاه ترا چو خاک گرداند پست   می نوش بخرمی که این چرخ کهن

۲۸

نتوان بامید شک همه عمر نشست   چون نیست حقیقت ویقین اندردست

در بیخبری مردچه هشیار وچه مست   هان تا ننهیم جام می از کف دست

30

The dust under the feet of any fool,
Is the palm of a beloved, and the face of a
sweetheart.
Every brick on a palace battlement,
Is the finger of a minister, or the head of a king.

31

When the creator embellished the forms of nature,
Why did he condemn them to defeat and failure?
If they came out well, why break them?
If they didn't, who is at fault?

32

Behind the veil of secrets, no one has access.
Of this arrangement, no one's soul is aware.
Save in the heart of dust, there is no abode.
Drink wine, for such tales are not short.[40]

33

I was sleeping, a wise person told me,
From sleep, no flower of joy bloomed for anyone.
Why do you do something similar to death?
Drink wine. It is under the ground that one must
sleep.

۳۰

خاكی كه بزير پای هر نادانی است   كف صنمی و چهره جانانی است

هر خشت كه بر كنگرهٔ ایوانی است   انگشت وزیر یا سر سلطانی است

۳۱

دارنده چو تركیب طبایع آراست   از بهر چه افكندش اندر كم و كاست

گر نیك آمد شكستن از بهر چه بود   ور نیك نیامد این صور عیب كراست

۳۲

در پردهٔ اسرار كسی را ره نیست   زین تعبیه جان هیچ كس آگه نیست

جز در دل خاك هیچ منزلگه نیست   می خور كه چنین فسانه ها كوته نیست

۳۳

در خواب بدم مرا خردمندی گفت   كز خواب كسی را گل شادی نشكفت

كاری چكنی كه با اجل باشد جفت   می خور كه بزیر خاك می باید خفت

49

34

The circle where our coming and going take place,
Has no beginning and no end in sight.
No one utters a word of truth to explain
Whence we come or to where we go.

35

In the spring season, by a field,
Should a houri-natured beloved give me a cup of
wine,
Although this would be considered bad by the public,
I would be lower than a dog if I mention
paradise.[41]

36

Embrace the moment, for you will be separated
from your soul.
You will go in the veil of annihilation's mysteries.
Drink wine, you don't know where you came from.
Be happy, you don't know where you will go.

37

Saqi, flowers and grass have become much joyful.
Embrace the moment, for next week they will be
dust.
Drink wine, pick a flower, for when you look again,
Flowers have become dust, and grass motes.

۳۴

او را نه بدایت نه نهایت پیداست   در دایرۀ که آمد و رفتن ماست

کاین آمدن از کجا! و رفتن بکجاست   کس می نزد دمی در این معنی راست

۳۵

یك ساغر می دهد مرا بر لب کشت   در فصل بهار اگر بتی حورسرشت

سگ بهزمن است اگر برم نام بهشت   هرچند بنزد عامه این باشد زشت

۳۶

در پردۀ اسرار فنا خواهی رفت   دریاب که از روح جدا خواهی رفت

خوش باش ندانی بکجا خواهی رفت   می نوش ندانی از کجا آمدۀ

۳۷

دریاب که هفته دگر خاك شده است   ساقی گل و سبزه بس طربناك شده است

گل خاك شده است و سبزه خاشاك شده است   می نوش و گلی بچین که تا در نگری

39

The season of flowers, by a stream, alongside a
field,
With two or three congenial friends and a houri-
natured beauty.
Bring forth the cup, for the morning wine drinkers
Are free from mosques, and indifferent to
synagogues.

41

They say paradise with the houris is sweet,
I say the juice of the grape is sweet,
Take this cash, and leave what is on credit.
The song of the kettledrum, from the distance, is
sweet.

42

I am told the drunk is destined to hell.
That is an erroneous saying, one cannot depend on
it.
If the lover and the drunk will be in hell,
Tomorrow you will see paradise [bare] as a hand's
palm.

43

I don't know at all whether he who created me,
Destined me to paradise or to ugly hell.
A cup, a beloved, a harp, by a field,
These three for me cash, for you, paradise on credit.

۳۹

بایک دوسه اهل و لعبتی‌حورسرشت   فصل‌گل وطرف جویبار و لب‌کشت

آسوده ز مسجدند و فارغ ز کنشت   پیش‌آر قدح که باده نوشان صبوح

۴۱

من میگویم‌که آب‌انگورخوش‌است   گویندکسان بهشت با حودخوشت

کآواز دهل شنیدن ازدورخوش‌است   این نقدبگیر ودست ازآن‌نسیه بدار

۴۲

قولی‌است‌خلاف‌دل درآن‌نتوان بست   گویند مرا که دوزخی باشد مست

فردا بینی بهشت همچون‌کف دست   گرعاشق ومیخواره بـدوزخ باشند

۴۳

از اهل بهشت کرد یا دوزخ زشت   من هیچ ندانم‌که مرا آنکه سرشت

این هرسه مرا نقد ترا نسیه بهشت   جامی و بتی و بـربطی برلب‌کشت

44

Moonlight has torn, with light, the skirt of the
night.
Drink wine, a moment better than this, one cannot
find.
Be happy, and don't think that often the moon
Will shine on [our] graves one by one.

45

To drink wine and to be happy is my way of life.
To be indifferent to blasphemy and religion is my
religion.
I said to the world's bride: "What is your dowry?"
[She] said: "Your cheerful heart is my dowry."

46

Wine is melted ruby, and the jug is the mine.
The cup is the body, and its soul is wine.
That crystal cup filled with sparkling wine,
Is a tear hiding [our] sorrows.

47

Drink wine, for eternal life is this.
The gain from the time of your youth is this.
In the season of flowers, wine, and drunken friends,
Be happy for a moment, for life is this.

۴۴

می نوش دمی بهتر ازاین نتوان یافت مهتـاب بنور دامـن شب بشکافت

اندرسرخاك يك بیك خـواهد تافت خوش باش ومیندیش که مهتاب بسی

۴۵

فارغ بودن ز کفرودین دین من است می خوردن وشاد بودن آئین من است

گفتا دل خرم تو کابین من است گفتم بعروس دهر کابین تو چیست

۴۶

جسم است پیاله وشرابش جان است می لعل مذاب است وصراحی کان است

اشکی است که خون دل دراو پنهان است آن جام بلورین که زمی خندان است

۴۷

خود حاصلت ازدور جوانی این است می نوش که عمر جاودانی این است

خوش باش دمی که زندگانی این است هنگام گل و باده و یاران سرمست

48

The good and evil in the nature of man.
The joy and sorrow in destiny and fate.
Don't attribute them to the world. In the light of reason,
The world is a thousand times more helpless than you.

49

Red tulips growing in every field,
Owe their color to the red blood of a king.
Every stem of violet springing from the earth,
Is a mole that was on a sweetheart's face.

50

Every bit in the dust of a land,
Was a crown and a jewel before me and you.
Wipe gently the dust off a lovely face,
For that too was the beautiful face of a lovely one.

51

Every grass springing on the bank of a stream,
Sprung, so to speak, from the lips of an angel-tempered beauty.
So, do not step scornfully upon the grass,
For that grass sprung from the dust of a tulip-faced beauty.

۴۸

نیکی و بدی که در نهاد بشر است   شادی و غمی که درقضا و قدر است

باچرخ مکن حواله کاندر ده عقل   چرخ ازتو هزاربار بیچاره تر است

۴۹

دردهر دشتی که لاله زاری بوده است   ازسرخی خون شهریاری بوده است

هر شاخ بنفشه کز زمین میروید   خالی است که بررخ نگاری بوده است

۵۰

هردره که دردخاک زمینی بوده است   پیش ازمن وتو تاج ونگینی بوده است

گرد ازرخ نازنین بآزرم فشان   کانهم رخ خوب نازنینی بوده است

۵۱

هرسبزه که برکنارجوئی رسته است   گوئی زلب فرشته خوئی رسته است

پا بر سر سبزه تا بخواری ننهی   کان سبزه زخاك لاله روئی رسته است

52

A drink of wine is better than the kingdom of
Kavus,
Better than the throne of Qobad and the realm of
Tus.[42]
Every sigh that a libertine makes at dawn,
Is better than the worship of devout hypocrites.

53

When life draws to an end, let it be sweet or bitter.
When the cup is full, let it be in Baghdad or Balkh.
Drink wine, for after me and you, often the moon
Will go from new moon to old, and from old to new.

54

Those who mastered all knowledge and disciplines,
In all sciences became the light of scholars,
Found no way out of this dark night.
They told a tale, and sank into slumber.

56

Those who grew old, and those who are young,
Are all running toward their goal.
This old world will not remain for anyone.
They left, we shall leave, and others will come and
leave.

۵۲

یك جرعهٔ می ز ملك كاوس بهست   از تخت قباد و ملكت طوس بهست

هر ناله كه رندی بسحرگاه زنـد   از طـاعت زاهدان سالـوس بهست

۵۳

چون عمر بسر رسد چه شیرین وچه تلخ   پیمانه چو پر شود چه بغداد وچه بلخ

می نوش كه بعد از من وتو ماه بسی   از سلخ بغـره آیـد از غره بسلخ

۵۴

آنانكه محیط فضل و آداب شدند   در جمع كمال شمع اصحاب شدند

ره زین شب تاریك نبردند برون   گفتند فسانـهٔ و در خـواب شدند

۵۶

انهاكه كهن شدند واینها كـه نوند   هر كس بمراد خویش یك تك بدوند

این كهنه جهان بكس نماند باقی   رفتند و رویم و دیـگر آیند و روند

59

The [celestial] bodies dwelling in this palace,[43]
Create doubts for scholars.
Beware that you do not err in your reasoning,
For those who are competent are perplexed.

60

My coming has brought no gain to the world,
And my leaving will not increase its glory and
dignity.
And my two ears have not heard from anyone,
For what purpose were my coming and my
leaving.

62

Alas! [Life] capital ran out of [our] hands,
And because of death many hearts are filled with
sorrow.
No one returned from the other world that I may
ask,
How was the condition of travelers from this world.

63

Alas! The book of youth came to an end,
And the fresh spring of life became winter.
That bird of joy whose name was youth,
Alas! I know not when it came, when it left.

۵۹

اجرام که ساکنان این ایوانند   اسباب تردد خردمندانند

هان تا سر رشته خردگم نکنی   کانانکه مدبرند سرگردانند

۶۰

از آمدنم نبود گردون را سود   وزرفتن من جلال و جاهش نفزود

وز هیچ کسی نیز دو گوشم نشنود   کاین آمدن و رفتنم از بهرچه بود

۶۲

افسوس که سرمایه زکف بیرون شد   وزدست اجل بسی‌جگرها خون شد

کس نامد ازآن جهان که پرسم ازوی   کاحوال مسافران دنیا چون شد

۶۳

افسوس که نامهٔ جوانی طی شد   وان تازه بهار زندگانی دی شد

آن مرغ طرب که نام او بودشباب   فریاد ندانم که کی آمدکی شد

64

For a long time we will not be, and the world will be.
Our name will not be, nor any trace of us.
Before this, we were not, and nothing was out of
order.
Hereafter, when we will not be, all will be the same.

65

Reason searching the road to happiness,
Tells you a hundred times a day,
Enjoy this one moment of your time, for you are not
A leek that after being reaped, grows again.

66

How surprisingly [fast] life's caravan is passing!
Embrace the moment that with joy is passing.
Saqi, why worry about [our] adversaries tomorrow?
Bring forth the cup, for the night is passing.

67

My back is being bent by time,
And no task can I accomplish well.
My soul resolved to make a journey, and I
mentioned it.
It said, what can I do, the house is falling down.

۶۴

اى بس كه نباشيم وجهان خواهد بود نى نام زما و نى نشان خواهد بود

زين پيش نبوديم ونبد هيچ خلل زين‌پس چونباشيم همان خواهد بود

۶۵

اين عقل كه در ره سعادت پويد روزى صد بار خود ترا ميگويد

درياب تو اين يكدم وقتت كه نۀ آن تره كه بدروند و ديگر رويد

۶۶

اين قافلۀ عمر عجب ميگذرد درياب دمى كه با طرب ميگذرد

ساقى غم فرداى حريفان چه‌خورى پيش آر پياله را كه شب ميگذرد

۶۷

بر پشت من از زمانه تو مى‌آيد وزمن همه كار نانكو مى‌آيد

جان عزم رحيل كرد و گفتم بمرو گفتا چكنم خانه فرو مى‌آيد

70

Since they make destiny write my fate without me,
Why do they hold me responsible for the good and
bad of it?
Yesterday without me, and today, like yesterday,
without me and you.
Tomorrow for what reason before the judge will
they call me?

71

How long will you be a prisoner of color and scent?
How long will you pursue every evil and good?
Whether you are the spring of Zamzam[44] or the
water of life,
At the end you will sink into the heart of dust.

73

Since Venus and the moon appeared in the sky,
Better than clear wine nothing has been seen.
I am surprised at wine merchants, for
Better than what they sell, what will they buy?

76

In the world, when they strike the song of the new
flower,
Command, O beloved, that they bring enough
wine.
Be free of houris, castles, paradise and hell,
Since many rumors are spread about them.

۷۰

بـرمن قلم قضا چو بـی من دانند   پس نيك و بدش زمن چرا ميدانند

دی بی من وامروز چودی بی من و تو   فـردا بچه حجتم بـداور خوانند

۷۱

.تاچند اسير رنگ و بو خواهی شد   چند ازپی هرزشت ونکو خواهی شد

گر چشمهٔ زمزمی وگر آب حیات   آخـربدل خـاك فروخواهـی شد

۷۳

تا زهره ومه درآسمان گشت پدید   بهتر زمـی نـاب كسی هیچ نـدید

مـن دردعجبـم ز میفروشان كایشان   بهزانكه فروشند چه خواهند خرید

۷۶

در دهرچـو آواز گـل تازه دهند   فرمـای بتا كه مـی باندازه دهند

از حور و قصور وزبهشت و دوزخ   فارغ بنشین كه آن هرآوازه دهند

77

In the world, he who has half a loaf of bread,
Who has a nest for resting,
Is neither the master nor the servant of anyone,
Tell [him] to live happily, for his is a happy world.

79

It is a fair day, and the air is neither warm nor cold.
The cloud is washing the dust from the flower-
bed's face.
The nightingale, in its own tongue, is crying out
To the yellow flower that one must drink wine.

80

Before being attacked by surprise, at night,
Command that they bring the rose-colored wine.
You are not gold, O heedless fool,
To be put in the ground, and brought out again.

82

No one has resolved the secrets of death.
No one has taken one step beyond nature.
I observe, from apprentice to master,
Failure in everyone born of a mother.

۷۷

از بهــر نشست آشیانــی دارد   در دهر هر آنکه نیم نــانــی دارد

گو شادبزی‌که خوش جهانی دارد   نه خــادم‌کس بود نه مخدوم کسی

۷۹

ابــر از رخ گلــزار همی شویــد گــرد   روزی است خوش‌وهواله‌گرم‌است ونه‌سرد

فریاد همی‌کند‌که مــی باید خورد   بلبل بزبان حال خود با گل زدد

۸۰

فرمــای‌که تــا باده گلگون آرند   زان‌پیش‌که برسرت شبیخون آرند

در خاك نهند و باز بیرون آرنــد   تــو زدن‌ئای غــافل نادان كــه ترا

۸۲

کس یك قدم از نهاد بیرون ننهاد   کس مشکل اسرار اجل را نگشاد

عجز است بدست هرکه ازمادر زاد   من مینگــرم ز مبتدی تــا استــاد

83

Lessen your greed for the world, and live happily.
Break ties with the world's good and evil.
Take in [your] hand [a cup of] wine, and a sweet-
heart's locks.
For this too will pass soon, and not remain long.

84

Although my grief and suffering have been lasting,
Your pleasure and joy have been rising.
Rely on neither, for the revolution of the sky
Has behind the veil a thousand kinds of games.

85

The revolving world brings forth no flower from
the earth,
That it doesn't break and deposit again in the earth.
If clouds absorbed dust as they do water,
Blood of dear ones would rain till resurrection day.

87

They say there will be paradise and houris.
Wine, milk, and honey will be there.
If we chose wine and sweethearts, why fear?
Since thus will be the outcome of the affair.

٨٣

کم کن طمع ازجهان ومیزی خودسند   وزنیك و بد زمانـه بكسل پیوند

می درکف وزلف دلبری گیر که زود   هم بگذرد و نماند این روزی چند

٨٤

گرچـه غم ودنج من درازی دارد   عیش و طـرب تو سرفرازی دارد

برهر دو مکن تکیه که دوران فلك   در پرده هزار گونه بازی دارد

٨٥

گردون ز زمین هیچ گلی بر نارد   کش نشکند و هـم بزمین نسپارد

گر ابر چو آب خاك را بر دارد   تـا حشر همه خون عزیزان بارد

٨٧

گویند بهشت وحودعین خواهدبود   آنجامی وشیروانگبین خواهد بود

گرما می ومعشوق گزیدیم چـه باك   چون عاقبت کار چنین خواهد بود

88

They say there will be paradise, houris, and
Kowsar.
Streams of wine, milk, honey, and sugar.
Fill the cup of wine and set [it] in my hand.
Cash is better than a thousand "on credit."

89

They say those who are virtuous,
Will be thus resurrected after they die.
We are continuously with wine and sweethearts,
So on resurrection day, we would be thus resurrected.

90

Drink wine, for it relieves [your] heart
From all worries and pains in the world.
Abstain not from an elixir of which
A sip relieves a thousand ills.

92

Every morning when the dew covers the tulip's
face,
The voilet's stature bends in the meadow.
Indeed I take delight in the rosebud,
For it gathers its skirt about it.

٨٨

جوی می و شیرو شهد وشکر بـاشد   گـویند بهشت و حور و کوثر باشد

نقدی ز هـزار نسیه خوشتر باشد   پر کن قدح بـاده و بر دستم نـه

٨٩

زانسان که بمیرند چنان برخیزند   گویند هـر آنکسان که با پرهیزند

باشد که بحشرمان چنان انگیزند   مـا با مـی و معشوقه از آنیم مدام

٩٠

و انـدیشه هفتـاد و دو ملت بیـرد   می خورد که زدل قلت و کثرت ببرد

یك جـرعه خوری هزار علت ببرد   پـرهیز مکن زکیمیائی کـه از او

٩٢

بـالای بنفشه درچمن خـم گیرد   هر صبح کـه رویلالـه شبنم گیرد

کو دامـن خویشتن فراهم گیرد   انصاف مـرا ز غنچه خـوش میـآید

93

Never has my heart been deprived of knowledge.
Few secrets remain that have not been resolved.
For seventy-two years I reflected day and night.
It became clear to me that nothing has been resolved.

94

The seed of hope in the harvest will remain,
The garden and the house, without you and me, will remain.
Your silver and gold, from a coin to a grain,
Enjoy them with a friend, or for the enemy they will remain.

95

Congenial friends have all been lost.
They have been, one by one, humbled by death.
We drank the same wine in the feast of life.
Two or three rounds before us, they got drunk.

97

There was a drop of water, it disappeared into the sea,
An atom of dust, it vanished into the earth.
What are your coming and going in this world?
A fly appeared and disappeared.

٩٣

کم ماند ز اسرارکه معلوم نشد هر گز دل من ز علم محروم نشد

معلومم شد که هیچ معلوم نشد هفتادودوسال فکرکردم شب وروز

٩٤

هم باغ وسرای بی تو ومن ماند هم دانهٔ امید بخرمن ماند

با دوست بخورگرنه بدشمن ماند سیم وزدخویش از دِرَمی تابجوی

٩٥

درپای اجل یکان‌یکان پست شدند یاران موافق همه ازدست شدند

دوری دوسه پیشتر زما مست شدند خوردیم زیك شراب در مجلس عمر

٩٧

یك ذرهٔ خاك با زمین یکتا شد یك قطره آب بود با دریا شد

آمد مگسی پدید و ناپیدا شد آمد شدن تو اندرین عالم چیست

73

98

If a man could have bread for two days,
And a drink of fresh water from a broken jug.
The servant of a lesser man, why should one be?
Or someone like oneself, why should one serve?

99

Bring that ruby [colored wine] in a plain glass.
Bring that confidant and companion of every free
soul.
Since you know that the duration of this world of
dust,
Is that of a wind that passes fast, bring the wine.

100

For what will be, O friend, why are you grieved?
Your heart and soul deep in vain thoughts.
Live happily and spend [life] with joy.
You were not consulted at the start of the affair.

103

O my heart, imagine all things in the world accord-
ing to your wish.
Imagine the garden of your joy embellished with
verdure.
Then imagine, upon that verdure, like dew,
You sat one night, and rose in the morning.

٩٨

وزکـوزه شکستـهٔ دمـی آبی سرد   یك نـان بدودوزاگر بود حاصلِمد

یاخدمت چونخودی چرا بایدکرد   مأموركم ازخـودی چـرا باید بود

٩٩

وان محـرم و مونس هرآزاده بیـار   آن لعـل درآ بـگینهٔ سـاده بیـار

باد است که زودبگذرد باده بیـار   چـون میدانـی که مدت عالمخاك

١٠٠

وزفکـرت بیهوده دل و جان افكار   ازبـودنی ایدوست چه داری تیمار

تـدبیر نه با تـوکرده‌اند اول كار   خرم بزی و جهـان بشادی گذندان

١٠٢

بـاغ طـربت بسبزه آراسته‌گیر   ایدل همه اسباب جهان‌خواسته‌گیر

بنشسته و بـامداد بـرخاسته گیر   وآنگاه برآن سبزه شبی چون شبنم

75

104

These inhabitants of graves have turned into dirt and dust.
Each atom separated from the other.
Alas! What kind of wine is this, that till doomsday,
They are unconscious and unaware of all matters.

107

Yesterday I saw a potter in the bazaar,
Kicking repeatedly at a piece of clay.
And the clay, in a mute tongue, was saying to him,
I was like you, be kind to me.

108

Drink that wine which is eternal life.
Drink what is the capital of youth's delight.
Drink what burns like fire, but for sorrow,
Soothes like the water of life.

109

If you drink wine, drink it with wise men,
Or drink it with a tulip-faced, laughing sweetheart.
Don't drink much, don't make it a habit, don't divulge it.
Drink a little, drink now and then, and drink it in secret.[45]

۱۰۴

هر ذره ز هر ذره گرفتند کنار   این اهل قبور خاک گشتند و غبار

بیخود شده و بیخبرند از همه کار   آه این چه شراب است که تا روز شمار

۱۰۷

بر پاره گلی لگد همی زد بسیار   دی کوزه گری بدیدم اندر بازار

من همچو تو بوده‌ام مرا نیکودار   وآن گل بزبان حال با او میگفت

۱۰۸

سرمایهٔ لذت جوانی است بخور   زان می که حیات جاودانی است بخور

سازنده چو آب زندگانی است بخور   سوزنده چو آتش است لیکن غم را

۱۰۹

یا با صنمی لاله رخی خندان خور   گر باده خوری تو با خردمندان خور

اندک خور و گه گاه خور و پنهان خور   بسیار مخور ورد مکن فاش مساز

77

110

It is just before dawn, rise O young lad.
Fill the crystal cup with ruby-colored wine,
For you will seek much and not find again
This one borrowed instant, in this corner of annihi-
lation.

111

Of all those who left on that long road,
Who returned to tell us about the mystery?
So, on this crossroad of greed and need,
Leave nothing, for you will not return.

112

O wise old man, rise earlier at dawn,
And look sharply at that dust-sifting child.
Counsel him and tell him to sift gently
The brain of Kay-Qobad's head and Parviz's eyes.[46]

113

It is just before dawn, rise O source of coquetry.
Gently drink wine and play the harp,
For those who are here will not last long,
And of those who are gone, none will return.

١١٠

وقت سحراست خیز ای طرفه پسر پر باده لعل کن بلوریـن ساغر

کایـن یکدم عادیت دراین کنج فنا بسیار بجوئـی و نیابی دیـگر

١١١

از جملهٔ رفتگـان این راه دراز باز آمده کیست تا بما گـویدراز

پس بـرسر ایـن دوراههٔ آزونیاز تا هیچ نمانی که نمی آئی بـاز

١١٢

ای پیـر خـردمند پکه تر برخیز وان کودك خاك بیـز را بنگر تیـز

پندش دهو گو که نرم نرمك می بیز مغز سر کیقباد و چشم پرویز

١١٣

وقت سحر است خیز ای مایهٔ ناز نرمك نرمك باده خور و چنگ نواز

کانهـا کـه بجـایند نپـایند بسی وانهاکه شدند کس نمی آیـد باز

114

I saw a bird perched on the rampart of Tus,
Having laid before it the skull of Kay-Kavus,[47]
Saying to the skull: "Alas, alas! Where is
The ringing of bells, and where the lament of drums?

116

Khayyam, if you are drunk with wine, be happy.
If you are sitting with a moon-faced [beauty], be happy.
As the outcome of this world's affair is non-existence,
Imagine you are not, since you are, be happy.

117

Into the workshop of a potter, I walked yesterday,
I saw two thousand pots speaking and silent.
Suddenly one pot cried out:
Where is the pot-maker, the pot-buyer, the pot-seller?

119

From the layers of black mud to the top of Saturn,
I resolved all the main difficulties.
With cunning, I opened difficult knots,
Each knot has been opened save the knot of death.

۱۱۴

مرغــی دیــدم نشسته بربارهٔ طوس   در پیش نهـاده کلـه کیـکاوس

باکله همی‌گفت که افسوس افسوس   کوبانگ جرسها وکجا نالهٔ کوس

۱۱۶

خیام اگرزباده مستی خوش بـاش   باماه رخی اگر نشستی خوش باش

چـون عـاقبت‌کار جهـان نیستی‌است   انگارکه نیستی چو هستی‌خوش‌باش

۱۱۷

در کارگه کـوزه‌گری رفتم دوش   دیدم دو هزارکوزه گویـا وخموش

ناگاه یـکی کوزه برآورد خروش   کوکوزه‌گروکوزه خروکوزه‌فروش

۱۱۹

از جـرم گل سیاه تـا اوج زحـل   کردم همه مشکلات کلی را حـل

بکشادم بنـدهـای مشکل بحیـل   هـر بند گشاده شد بجز بند اجل

120

With a cypress-tall [beauty] fresher than a harvest
of flowers.
Don't leave the cup of wine and the flower's skirt,
Before suddenly by the wind of death,
The skirt of our life becomes like the flower's skirt.

121

O friend, come, let us not care for tomorrow,
Let us avail ourselves of this instant of life.
Tomorrow when we leave this transient world,
We will be face to face with seven thousand year-
olds.

123

Rise from sleep, that we may drink wine,
Before we have to endure pain from the world.
For this quarrelsome wheel suddenly one day,
Will not give us time for a drink of water.

127

Since our stay in this world is not permanent,
[To be] without wine and sweethearts is a great
error.
Till when hopes and fear of an eternal or created
world?[48]
When I am gone, let the world be created or eternal.

۱۲۰

از دست منه جام مـی و دامن گل   بـاسرو قدی تـازه‌تر ازخرمن گل

پیراهن عمر ما چو پیراهن گل   زان پیش که ناگه شود ازباد اجل

۱۲۱

ویـن یـکدم عمردا غنیمت شمریم   ای دوست بیاتـا غم فـردا نخوریم

بـا هفت هـزار سالگان سربسریم   فردا که از این دیرفنا درگذریم

۱۲۳

زان پیش که از زمانه تابی بخوریم   برخیز ذخـواب تا شرابی بخوریم

چندان ندهد زمان که آبی بخوریم   کاین چرخ ستیزه روی ناگه‌روزی

۱۲۷

پس بی‌می ومعشوق‌خطائی‌است عظیم   چون نیست مقام ما دراین دهر مقیم

چومن‌رفتم جهان چه‌محدث چه‌قدیم   تاکی زقـدیم و محدث امیدم و بیم

128

To hide the sun in the mud, I cannot.
To tell the world's secrets, I cannot.
From the sea of my reflection, reason brought forth
a pearl.
To disclose it, out of fear, I cannot.

129

The enemy said, incorrectly, that I am a philosopher.
God knows that what he said, I am not.
But since I have come to this nest of sorrow,
I have failed to know who I am.[49]

132

To live without clear wine, I cannot.
To carry my body's burden, without wine, I cannot.
I am the servant of that moment when the Saqi says:
"Take one more cup," and I cannot.

133

From time to time someone comes forth and
declares:
"It is I!"
With wealth, with silver and gold he comes and
declares:
"It is I!"
When his small business gets organized, suddenly
one day,
Death comes out of ambush and declares: "It is I!"

۱۲۸

خـورشید بـگل نهفت مـی‌نتوانم   و اسرار زمـانه گفت مـی‌نتوانم

از بحـر تفکـرم بـرآورد خـرد   دری کـه ز بیـم سفت مـی‌نتوانم

۱۲۹

دشمن بغلط گفت کـه مـن فلسفیم   ایـزد دانـد که آنچه او گفت نیـم

لیکن چو دریـن غم آشیان آمـدهام   آخر کم از آنکه من بدانم که کیم

۱۳۲

من‌بی مـی نـاب زیستن نتوانـم   بی‌باده‌کشید بـار تـن نتوانـم

من بنده‌ٔ آن دمـم که ساقی گوید   یک جام دگر بگیرو من نتوانم

۱۳۳

هر یک چندی یکی برآیـد که منم   بـانعمت و بـا سیم وزر آیدکه منم

چـون کارك او نظـام گیرد روزی   ناگه اجل از کمین درآید کـه منم

134

For a time in childhood, to a master we went.
For a time we were happy as masters ourselves.
Hear the end of the story, what happened to us.
From dust we rose and in the wind we went.

135

Not a day am I free from the world's chain.
Not a moment am I happy about my existence.
I have long been an apprentice of the world.
I am still not a master in the world's affairs.

136

When yesterday has passed, do not remember it.
Tomorrow has not come, do not complain.
Do not dwell on what has not come or what has
passed.
Be happy now and do not waste life.

137

O eye, if you are not blind, see the grave.
See this world full of trouble and anxiety.
Kings, chiefs and lords are under the mud.
See beautiful faces in the ant's mouth.

۱۳۴

یک چند بکودکی باستاد شدیم   یک چند باستادی خود شادشدیم

پایان سخن شنوکه ما را چه رسید   از خاک درآمدیم و برباد شدیم

۱۳۵

یک روز ز بند عالم آزادنیم   یکدم زدن از وجود خودشادنیم

شاگردی روزگار کردم بسیار   در کار جهان هنوز استادنیم

۱۳۶

ازدی که گذشت هیچ ازویاد مکن   فرداکه نیامده است فریاد مکن

بر نامده و گذشته بنیاد مکن   حالی خوش باش و عمربرباد مکن

۱۳۷

ای دیده اگر کور نه‌ای گور ببین   وین عالم پرفتنه و پرشور ببین

شاهان وسران وسروران زیر گلند   روهای چو مه در دهن مور ببین

138

Rise and do not grieve for the passing world.
Sit down and spend a moment with joy.
If there were fidelity in the world's essence,
Your turn [to live] would not have come.

142

To be content with a bone, like the vulture,
Is better than to be a parasite at an ignoble man's
table.
To be content with one's own barley bread is indeed
better
Than to be contaminated with the sweet drink of a
mean man.

143

Some people are pondering on the path of religion,
Some believe they are on the path of ceritude.
I fear that a voice may exclaim one day,
O unaware people, the path is neither here nor
there.

144

There is a bull in the sky, and its name is Pleiades.[50]
Another bull is hidden under the earth.
Open your wisdom's eyes. See, with certitude,
Under and above two bulls, a handful of
donkeys.[51]

۱۳۸

برخیز و مخور غم جهان گذران   بنشین و دمی بشادمانی گذران

در طبع جهان اگر وفائی بودی   نوبت بتو خود نیامدی از دگران

۱۴۲

قانع بیک استخوان چو کرکس بودن   بهزانکه طفیل خوان ناکس بودن

بانان جوین خویش حقا که بهاست   کالوده بیالوده هرخس بودن

۱۴۳

قومی متفکرند اندر ره دین   قومی بگمان فتاده درراه یقین

میترسم از آنکه بانگ آید روزی   کای بیخبران راه نه آنست ونه این

۱۴۴

گاوی است در آسمان و نامش پروین   یک گاو دگر نهفته در زیر زمین

چشم خردت باز کن از دوی یقین   زیرو زبر دوگاو مشتی خرین

145

If I could, like God, lay hand on the celestial sphere,
I would eliminate this sphere.
Anew I would build another sphere.
So that a free man could easily fulfill his heart's desire.

147

Drinking wine and being around fair ones,
Is better than practicing devotion with hypocrisy.
If the lover and the drunkard will be in hell,
Then no one will see the face of paradise.

149

That palace that emulated the [celestial] wheel,
Against whose portal, kings put their faces,[52]
We saw a turtledove perched on its battlement, saying,
Where [are they], where, where, where?

151

When from our bodies have departed my pure soul and yours,
They will lay a couple of bricks on my grave and yours.
Then for the bricks of others' graves,
In a mold they will pour my dust and yours.

۱۴۵

گر بر فلکم دست بدی چون یزدان   برداشتمی من این فلك را زمیان

و ز نو فلکی دگر چنان ساختمی   کازاده بکام دل رسیدی آسان

۱۴۷

می خوردن و گرد نیکوان گردیدن   به ز آنکه بزرق زاهدی ورزیدن

گر عاشق ومست دوزخی خواهد بود   پس روی بهشت کس نخواهد دیدن

۱۴۹

آن قصر که بر چرخ همی زد پهلو   بر درگه او شهان نهادندی رو

دیدیم که بر کنگره اش فاخته   بنشسته همی گفت که کو کو کو کو

۱۵۱

از تن چو برفت جان پاك من وتو   خشتی دو نهند بر مغاك من و تو

وانگاه برای خشت گور دگران   در کالبدی کشند خاك من وتو

152

Drink wine, since destiny, for my destruction and
yours,
Has an intention against my pure soul and yours,
Sit on the verdure and drink clear wine,
For this verdure will often spring from my dust and
yours.

154

Look, the flower's skirt has been torn by the zephyr.
The nightingale has become cheerful by the
flower's beauty.
Sit in the shade of the flower, for often this flower
Will fall on the dust, and we have turned into dust.

155

Till when will I worry whether I have or have not.
Whether I will spend this life happily or not.
Fill the cup of wine, for it is not clear to me,
Whether this breath I inhale, I shall exhale or not.

157

Of the world's wealth whatever you eat or wear,
You are excused if you strive to obtain it.
All the rest is worthless, beware,
Do not sell precious life for it.

۱۵۲

قصدی دارد بجان پاك من و تو   می خورکه فلك بهر هلاك من وتو

کاین سبزه بسی دمد ز خاك من وتو   در سبزه نشین و میروشن میخور

۱۵۴

بلبل ز جمال گل طربناك شده   بنگر ز صبا دامن گل چاك شده

دمی خاك فرو ریزد وما خاك شده   درسایهٔ گل نشین که بسیار این گل

۱۵۵

وین عمر بخوشدلی گذارم یا نه   تاکی غم آن خورم که دارم یا نه

کایندم که فرو برم برآرم یا نه   پر کن قدح باده که معلوم نیست

۱۵۷

معذوری اگر در طلبش میکوشی   آن مایه ز دنیا که خوری یاپوشی

تا عمر گرانبها بدان نفروشی   باقی همه رایگان نیرزد هشدار

93

158

By the coming of spring and the parting of winter,
The leaves of our existence are being folded.
Drink wine and grieve not, for the wise have said,
The world's sorrows are poison, and their antidote
is wine.

159

From a potter I once bought a jug.
That jug told all kinds of secrets.
I was a king having a golden cup.
Now I have become any drunkard's jug.

160

O you who are the result of four and seven,
Who are excited, I know, about seven and four.[53]
Drink wine, for I told you a thousand times before.
There is no return, when you are gone, you are
gone.

161

O [my] heart, you will not penetrate the enigma's
secrets,
Nor the subtleties of shrewd learned people.
Here, with ruby-colored wine, build a paradise.
For there, where paradise is, you may or may not
reach.

۱۵۸

اوراق وجود ما همی گردد طـی   از آمدن بهار و از رفتن دی

غمهای جهان‌چو زهر وتریاقش می   می‌خور مخوراندوه که فرمودحکیم

۱۵۹

آن‌کوزه سخن‌گفت ز هر اسراری   از کوزه گری کوزه خریدم باری

اکنون شده‌ام کـوزه هـر خماری   شاهی بودم که جام زدینم بـود

۱۶۰

وزهفت و چهار دائّم اندر تفتی   ای آنـکه نتیجهٔ چهـار و هفتی

باز آمدنت نیست چـو رفتی دفتی   می‌خور که هزار بار پیشت گفتم

۱۶۱

در نکته زیـرکان دانـا نـرسی   ای دل تـو باسرار معمـا نرسی

کانجاکه بهشت است دسی یا نرسی   این جا بمی لعل بهشتی میساز

162

O friend, of truth, hear a word from me.
Be with ruby-colored wine and a silver-bodied
[beauty].
For he who made the world, cares not
For the moustache of someone like you, and the
beard of someone like me.

163

I wish there were a place for resting,
Or a destination to this long road.
I wish, after a hundred thousand years, there were
hope
Of springing, like grass, from the heart of dust.

164

Last night I hit an earthen jug against a rock.
I was drunk when I commited that mischievous act.
In its mute tongue, the jug spoke to me,
I was like you, you too will be like me.

166

Take a cup and a jug, O kind one.
Sit carefree by a field, on the bank of a stream.
Many a dear person this ill-tempered wheel
Has made a hundred times into a cup, a hundred
times into a jug.

۱۶۲

با باده لعل باش و با سیم تنی   ای دوست حقیقت شنو از من سخنی

از سبلت چون توئی وریش چومنی   کانکس که جهان کرد فراغت دارد

۱۶۳

یا این ره دور را رسیدن بودی   ای کاش که جای آرمیدن بودی

چون سبزه امید بـر دمیدن بودی   کاش از پی صدهزار سال ازدل خاک

۱۶۴

سرمست بدم چو کردم این اوباشی   بـر سنگ زدم دوش سبوی کاشی

من چون تو بدم تو نیز چون من باشی   با من بزبان حال میگفت سبو

۱۶۶

فارغ بنشین بکشته زادولب جوی   برگیر پیاله و سبوای دلجوی

صدبار پیاله کرد و صد بار سبوی   بس شخص عزیزراکه چرخ بدخوی

167

I saw an old man in a tavern.
I said, will you not tell about the departed ones?
Drink wine, he said, for many like us departed,
And there hasn't been any news about them.

168

Till when the tale of five and four,[54] O Saqi.
Let it be one or a hundred thousand problems,
O Saqi.
We are all dust, play the harp, O Saqi.
We are all wind, bring the wine, O Saqi.

169

In every direction I look,
A stream from Kowsar is running through the garden.
The field is like paradise, speak less of Kowsar.
Sit in paradise with a paradise-faced [beauty].

171

I walked into the workshop of a potter.
At the foot of the wheel, I saw the master standing,
Molding on the pot a handle and a head,
From the hand of a beggar, and the head of a king.

۱۶۷

گفتم نـکنی ز رفتگـان اخباری   پیـری دیـدم بخـانـهٔ خمـادی

رفتند و خبـر بـاز نیامد باری   گفتا می‌خون که همچو ما بسیادی

۱۶۸

مشکلچه یکی چه صدهزارایساقی   تا چند حدیث پنج و چادای ساقی

بادیم همه باده بیار ای ساقی   خاکیم همه چنگ بساز ای‌ساقی

۱۶۹

دربـاغ دوان است ز کوثر جوئی   چندانـکه نـگاه میـکنم هـرسوئی

بنشیـن بـه بهشت بـا بهشتی روئی   صحراچوبهشت است ز کوثرکم‌گوی

۱۷۱

در پایهٔ چرخ دیـدم استاد بپای   در کارگه کوزه گری کردم رای

از کله پـادشاه و از دست گـدای   میکرد دلیر کـوزه را دسته و سر

172

In my heart's ear, the celestial wheel secretly said,
You attribute to me the verdict of destiny.
If I had any control over my own revolution,
I would liberate myself from wandering.

173

From that jug of wine in which there is no harm,
Fill up a bowl, drink it, give me one,
Before, O beloved, on a roadside,
A potter molds into a jug my dust and yours.

175

If one could have a loaf of wheat bread,
About two liters of wine, a mutton's thigh,
With a tulip-faced [beauty], in a garden.
That would be a pelasure not within the reach of
any sultan.

177

Beware, O potter! Watch out if you are aware.
How long will you despise people's clay?
You have laid, on the wheel, Fereidun's finger,
And Kay-Khusraw's[55] hand. What is on your mind?

۱۷۲

در گوش دلم گفت فلک پنهانی   حکمی که قضا بود ز مـن میدانی

در گردش خویش اگر مرا دست بدی   خود را برهاندمی ز سرگردانی

۱۷۳

زان کوزهٔ می که نیست دروی ضرری   پر کن قدحی بخور بمن ده دگری

زان پیشتر ای صنم که در رهگذری   خاک من و تو کوزه کند کوزه گری

۱۷۵

گر دست دهـد ز مغز گندم نـانی   و زمـی دو منی ز گوسفندی دانی

با لالـه رخـی و گـوشهٔ بستانی   عیشی بود آن نـه حد هر سلطانی

۱۷۷

هان کوزه گرا پای اگر هشیاری   تـا چند کنی بر گل مردم خواری

انگشت فریـدون و کف کیخسرو   بر چرخ نهـادهٔ چـه می پنداری

178

At the time of the morning draught, O auspicious
beloved,
Play a melody and bring forth the wine,
For this coming of summer and departing of winter,
Has thrown in the dust hundreds of thousands of
Jams and Kays.[56]

۱۷۸

بــرساز تــرانهٔ و پیش آور مــی   هنگام صبوح ای صنم فــرخ پــی

ایــن آمــدن تیر مــه ورفتن دی   کافکند بخاك صدهزاران جم وکی

NOTES

1. The quatrains are arranged in the traditional Persian way of grouping verses according to the last letter of the last word of the verse, first those verses ending with the letter *a*, followed by those ending with the letter *b*, and so on.

2. At the present time, in the neighborhood of the town of Nayshaboor, a little over a mile from the tomb of Khayyam, there is a small village called Ma'amuri, where one finds a garden called Baq-i Khayyam (Garden of Khayyam). This garden must have belonged to Khayyam, and he probably lived there. See Sa'id Nafici, "Do Taqrir az Khajeh Imam Omar Khayyam" (Two Articles by Khajeh Imam Omar Khayyam), in *Majeleh Sharq* (Sharq Review), Month of Azar, A. H.1310 (November, 1931), p. 642.

3. Mohammad Ali Forooqi and Qani, *The Rubaiyat* (Tehran: Ranguin, A.H. 1321 [A.D. 1942] p. 2. For the text of Sanai's letter, see Nizami Aruzi Samarqandi, *Chahar Maqaleh* (Four Discourses), edited by Mohammad Mo'in (Tehran: Zavvar, A.H. 1333 [A.D. 1954]), Section Ta'aliqat (Supplements), pp. 296–300.

4. Edward G. Browne, *A Literary History of Persia* (Cambridge: the University Press, 1951), Vol.2, pp 246–247.

5. Ibid., p. 251.

6. Ibid., pp. 249–250.

7. Ibid., p. 250.

8. The original text of this treatise and its Persian translation are reproduced in the *Majeleh Sharq*, Month of Mordad, A.H. 1310 (August 1931), pp. 449–459.

9. See *Jabr o Moqabeleh Khayyam* (Algebra of Khayyam), edited by Gholam Hussein Mosahib (Tehran: Markazi, A.H. 1317 [1938]), pp. 200–204.

10. The numbers in parenthesis, both in the text and following each quatrain, are the numbers of the quatrains in this edition and in Forooqi's edition.

11. See *Majeleh Sharq*, Month of Azar, A.H. 1310 (November 1931), p. 649. (The translation is mine.)

12. The "houris" are the dark-eyed beauties of the Muslim paradise.

13. *Saqi* means cupbearer.

14. Referring to discussions about the world being created or eternal.

15. *Rasa'el Khayyam, No-Rooz Nameh, Resaleh Vojud* (Treatises of Khayyam, Book of the New Day, Treatise on Existence), edited by Avesta (Tehran: Zavvar, n.d.), vol. 1, p. 108 (The translation is mine.)

16. *No-Rooz Nameh, op., cit.*, pp.104–107. (The free translation is mine.)

17. In quatrain 109, Khayyam warns, however, that one should drink wine in the company of wise men, drink it now and then, and not make it a habit.

18. The idea in the *Rubaiyat* of human atoms coming again to life in pots, plants, etc., has also been mentioned by Sadeq Hedayat, in his edition of the *Rubaiyat* (Tehran: Amir Kabir, A.H. 1334, 1955).

19. Kowsar is a river in the Muslim paradise.

20. The words in brackets do not appear in the Persian text. They are added for clarity.

21. The word rendered by "beautiful" is the Persian word for "moon." In Persian, moon is often synonymous with beautiful, and the repetition of the word moon (*mah* in Persian) in this verse produces a pleasant effect in the Persian text.

22. Sometimes wine cups are made of silver or copper, and verses in praise of wine are carved on them.

23. The Persian text of the last verse is quite picturesque. It reads: "A hundred mouthfuls you eat of which wine is the slave." Wine being forbidden by the Koran, drinking wine is considered a sin, and Forooqi explains, in a note, that here the intention is to draw attention to the fact that drinking wine is not the only sin, there are many other sins that people commit without realizing that those sins are worse than wine drinking.

24. "Ruinous corner" meaning the world.

25. The ancient belief being that the world was made of those four elements, this quatrain means that we do not care for the world. (Forooqi's note. He adds also that he has a slight doubt about this quatrain being by Khayyam.)

26. Jamshid or Jam (The ending "shid" means bright, brilliant) is the famous king of the mythical Pishdadi dynasty of Iran who is known to have had a cup in which the entire world could be seen. It is also said that it was during Jamshid's reign that wine was discovered. In poetry, the cup of Jamshid (Jam-e Jam) is often compared to the cup of wine (Jam-e may). *Jam* means "cup." *May* means "wine."

27. Bahram (a king of Iran's Sasanian dynasty) liked hunting onagers. One day while hunting, he disappeared and was never seen again. In this quatrain, there is a play on the words onager and grave, the Persian for both words being goor: "Bahram who caught 'goor' all [his] life,/ Did you see how 'goor' caught Bahram."

28. Taft is the name of a town.

29. Five senses, four elements, six directions, and seven planets. (Forooqi's note.)

30. "Precious gems" refer to human bodies.

31. For jamshid and Bahram, see notes 26 and 27. Also, in the first verse of this quatrain, the Persian text has the word *ablaq* (piebald). Poets have often compared day and night to a black and white horse (a piebald horse).

32. No-Rooz is the Iranian New Year that falls on the first day of spring.

33. Dey, the tenth month of the Iranian calendar or the first month of winter, refers also to winter. In this quatrain, the poet makes a contrast between spring (No-Rooz being the first day of spring) and winter (Dey being the first month of winter). Dey also means yesterday.

34. Since it is impossible to mold bricks on water, by using this image, the poet refers to unfounded and vain thoughts.

35. The synagogue is the place used by Jews for worship, and has nothing to do with idol worshippers. Writers and poets have often made that mistake, and considered the synagogue as the worshipping place of all non-Muslims. Here, the general meaning is that no one knows the truth about paradise and hell. (Forooqi's note.)

36. The last verse explains the "elements" mentioned in the first one.

37. See note 32.

38. The Ancients believed that there were several skies, but did not agree on their number. (Forooqi's note.)

39. "This ancient wheel" meaning the world.

40. "Such tales are not short" refers to vain and endless discussions and commentaries about the problems of existence.

41. Muslims consider dogs unclean animals.

42. Qobad and Kavus are two kings of the Kayani

dynasty of Iran (mythical period).

43. Here "palace" refers to the universe.

44. Zamzam is a well in Mecca.

45. Khayyam believes in the beneficial properties of wine. Drinking wine with moderation and in the company of wise men is, therefore, beneficial, but since wine is forbidden by the Koran, Khayyam says that one should not drink it in public.

46. For Kay-Qobad see note 42. Khusraw Parviz is one of the kings of the Sasanian dynasty of Iran.

47. For kay-Kavus see note 42. Tus is a town.

48. "Eternal or created" refers to the philosophical discussions about the world being created or eternal. (Forooqi's note.)

49. Devout and narrow-minded people called philosophers "heretics" and tormented them. That is why Khayyam says that he is not a philosopher, but if he studies philosophy, it is because having come to this world, he wants to know who he is. (Forooqi's note.)

50. The Pleiades are a group of stars in the constellation Taurus (Bull), one of the signs of the Zodiac. For this reason the constellation was pictured as a bull in the sky. The other bull, mentioned in the second verse of this quatrain, is the bull that, according to ancient tales, carried the earth on its horn, and was standing on the back of a fish that was in the water. It is not said where the water was. Poets and writers have often referred to this tale. (Forooqi's note.)

51. "A handful of donkeys" refers to ignorant people. In Persian, an ignorant person is sometimes called a donkey.

52. The ancient Iranian Empire comprised many kingdoms. The kings of all these kingdoms paid allegiance to

the Shah of Iran. That is why the Shah of Iran has the title of Shahanshah, or king of kings.

53. Four elements and seven planets. (Forooqi's note.)

54. Five senses and four elements. (Forooqi's note.)

55. Fereidun, a king of the Pishdadi dynasty, Kay-Kavus, a king of the Kayani dynasty of Iran (mythical period).

56. Jams and Kays are Iranian kings. See notes 26, 55.